Great NEWSPAPER Crafts

Great NEWSPAPER Crafts

F. Virginia Walter

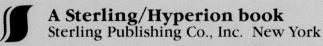

A Sterling/Hyperion book
Sterling Publishing Co., Inc. New York

A Sterling / Hyperion Book
First paperback edition published 1992
© 1991 by F. Virginia Walter

Sterling Publishing Company, Inc.
38 / Park Avenue South, New York, N.Y. 10016

Hyperion Press Limited
300 Wales Avenue, Winnipeg, MB, Canada R2M 2S9

Distributed in Canada by Sterling Publishing
% Canadian Manda Group, P.O. Box 920, Station U
Toronto, Ontario, Canada M8Z 5P9
Distributed in Great Britain and Europe by Cassell PLC
Villiers House, 41/47 Strand, London WC2N 5JE, England
Distributed in Australia by Capricorn Link Ltd.
P.O. Box 665, Lane Cove, NSW 2066

10   9   8   7   6   5   4   3   2

Illustrations by Teddy Cameron Long
Design by A. O. Osen
Typeset by Raeber Graphics Inc.

Contents

Introduction

The art of newspaper craft is the art of change. Creative children, and adults too, just like magicians, can transform old newspapers, boxes, paper bags, tubes, and other leftover materials into an entirely new form. Add a little imagination and the object becomes the maker's own work of art, the product of the maker's own self-expression.

Adults who like to make crafts find outlets for creative self-expression through the art of newspaper craft. The finished objects make wonderful gifts and can be undertaken as community projects or fund-raisers.

In my many years of teaching I have found that newspaper craft stimulates children to make unique and wonderful things as well. They enjoy the scope of the activity and it is simple enough for everyone to master. Children feel good about themselves through their accomplishments. They learn that changing one thing into another lets the old participate in and be a part of the new.

While the children are having so much fun recycling newspapers I use the opportunity to talk to them about other changes they might have noticed in their daily lives — new buildings where old ones once stood, new spring plants that replace the dead ones, nature's amazing metamorphosis of animals such as the butterfly or frog, and any other changes and renewals they suggest.

I have a bulletin board to display the newspaper crafts the children create. I usually mount the selections by topics on circles of colored paper and display them with humorous (if some-what corny) captions such as "A change is as good as a rest," "I've never met-a-morphosis I didn't like," "Changes are good for you," "If I can renew, you can too." Some simple projects are finished very quickly and can be displayed immediately. The children can tell stories about the cut-out dolls and the swords and shields they have made or make practical baskets and bowls to hold paper clips and pencils. Projects such as fish or animals can be undertaken by children in groups where each child elects to make one animal and then the collection is assembled in a cardboard fish tank or an imaginary jungle.

Papier-mâché is a bit more complicated because it takes time to dry. Big projects can be undertaken over a few days, as long as you have space to put the half-finished object where it won't be knocked about. Adults often create fascinating masks and marionettes. Of course children love these projects too, but need a little help. I have found that children enjoy the puppet theater. It takes time to make but the finished project allows hours of creative entertainment for children and adults. Newspaper craft provides pleasure and enjoyment for active minds and hands. It doesn't cost much to do and most of the materials can be found in your own home. I'm sure you'll find that all the projects are easy to make and as you begin working with old newspapers you may invent some new and exciting projects of your own.

From old to new, it's fun to do!

Materials and Tools

Not all materials or tools are needed for each project.

Newspapers

Working surface (old plastic table-cloth or newspapers)

Brown paper bags

Ice cream buckets for mixing and storing papier-mâché pulp

Stapler and staples

Clothespins or paper clips to hold projects in place while drying

Scissors with blunt, rounded ends

Glue and glue stick

Masking tape

Cellulose sticky tape

Shoelaces

String

Tissue paper in all colors

Colored construction paper

Felt-tipped markers

Pencils

Wallpaper paste (comes in powder form and must be mixed with water according to package instructions or buy it ready mixed)

Powdered poster paint

Purchased paint brushes in various sizes

An old muffin tin or plastic yogurt containers set in a shoebox to hold mixed paints

Shellac for waterproofing

Glitter, buttons, scraps of fur, cotton, yarn, twist ties, pipe cleaners, popsicle sticks, corks, paper tubes, cardboard boxes, fabric scraps, macaroni in various shapes and sizes, beads and sequins, old jewelry to decorate projects

Sardine tins, salmon cans, baking powder cans, small tins that do not have sharp edges

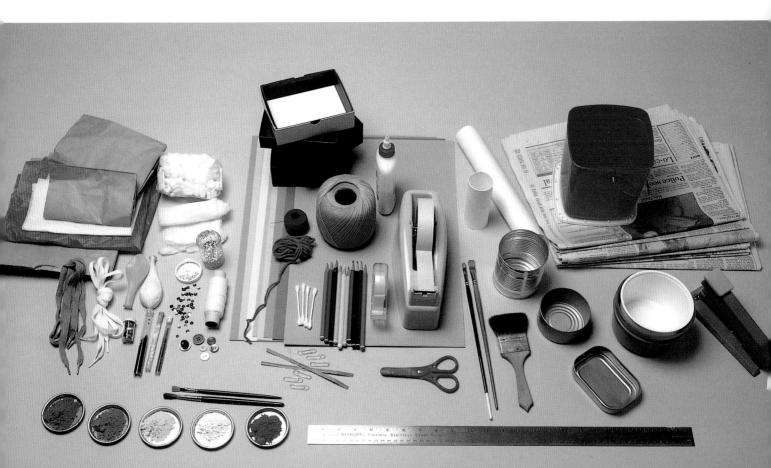

Basic Techniques

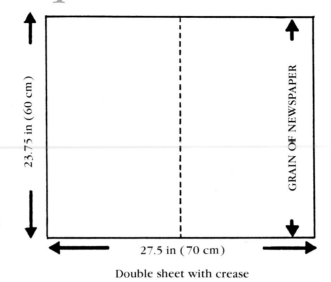

NEWSPAPER DIMENSIONS
used in this book
(Other sized newspapers can
also be used.)

23.75 in (60 cm)

27.5 in (70 cm)

GRAIN OF NEWSPAPER

Double sheet with crease

23.75 in (60 cm)

13.75 in (35 cm)

Single sheet

Tearing newspaper

Newspaper has a grain direction like
fabric. When making strips for your
projects, tear newspaper along the
grain of the paper — from the top of
the sheet to the bottom of the sheet.
A ruler edge can also be used.

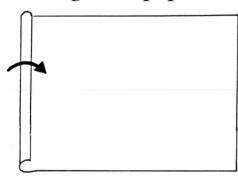

Grain of newspaper

Rolling newspaper

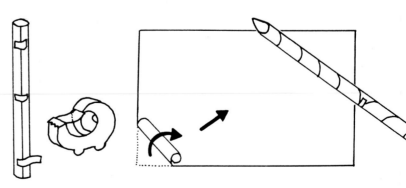

Method A PLAIN ROLL
Roll along length or width of a
newspaper sheet as needed. Tape
closed.

Method B DIAGONAL ROLL
Hold newspaper sheet at an angle.
Start at one corner and roll. Tape
as required.

8

Telescope method

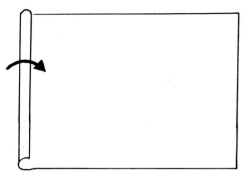

Roll a sheet of newspaper tightly from the short end to make a tube. Tape.

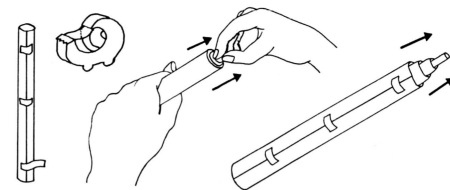

Hold the tube in one hand and with the other hand gently pull out inside roll as shown.

The tube will grow as you pull.

Newspaper cones

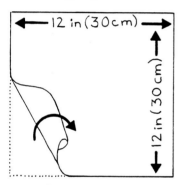

←—12 in (30 cm)—→

12 in (30 cm)

Cut a sheet of newspaper into a 12 in (30 cm) square. Starting one-quarter up one side, roll into a cone shape as shown and tape. To

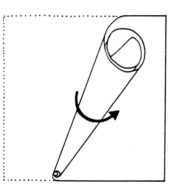

attach the cone to another surface, make cuts in the wide end, as shown. Tape or glue the cut tabs to the surface of the project. Vary

the size of the beginning newspaper square for larger or smaller cones.

Accordion pleating

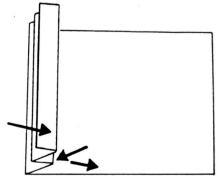

Cut a long strip of newspaper the desired width and length. Make folds back and forth (not over and over) until the strip is used up.

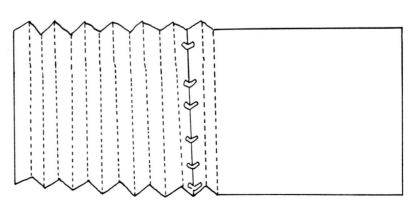

Tape another newspaper sheet to the edge of the first sheet if you want a longer pleated strip.

Continue folding.

Fringing

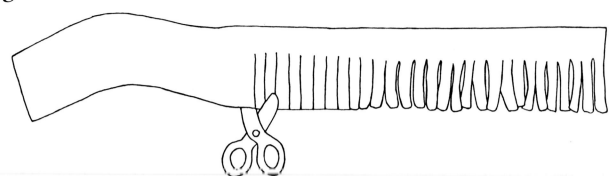

Cut a strip of newspaper as long and as wide as you desire the fringed band to be for your project.

Make cuts with a scissors along the edge to be fringed. Be sure you do not cut too close to the unfringed edge or the band will tear apart.

Vary the length of the cuts according to the desired depth of the fringe.

Curling

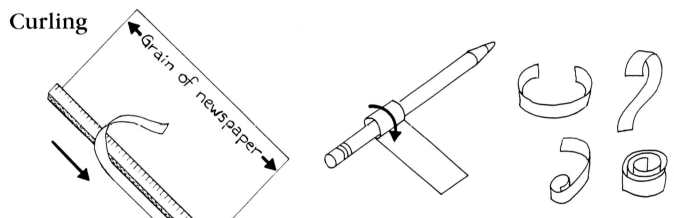

Place a single sheet of newspaper on a flat surface. Using a straight edge tear strips of newspaper along the grain of the newspaper as

shown. Wrap strips of newspaper around a pencil. How tightly you wrap the strip around the pencil will determine how curled the strip will be.

Crushed newspaper tubing

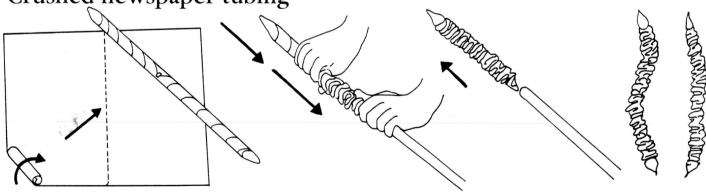

Roll a double sheet of newspaper diagonally into a loose tube. Tape the loose end. Grasp a pole, such as a broom handle, firmly 8 in (20

cm) from the top. With your other hand slide the tube over the pole and crush the newspaper, a little at a time, against the hand holding

the pole, until the entire tube is crushed. Slide the crushed tube from the pole as shown.

Catstairs

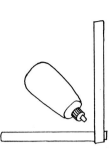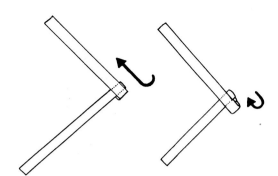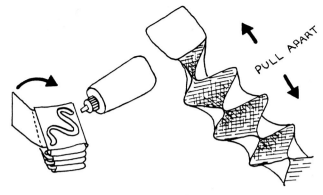

Cut 2 strips of newspaper as wide and as long as you need for the project. Place one end of one strip on top of the other strip at right

angles as shown. Glue at this point. Continue to fold one strip over the other, back and forth, maintaining the right angle to

make the desired length of catstair. Glue the ends together as shown. Pull catstairs apart gently and use in your project as required.

Button technique

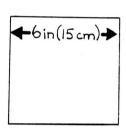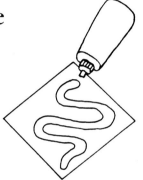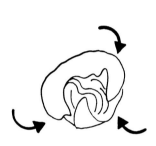

Depending on the project you need "buttons" for, make a square any size from a single sheet of newspaper. Spread glue on one

side of the newspaper square. Crumple the newspaper, glue side inward. Allow to dry.

Paint. Use for eyes, eggs, fruit, or centers of flowers.

Stuffing

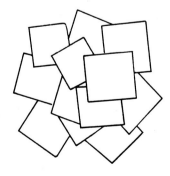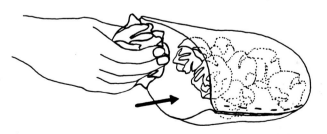

Tear a single sheet of newspaper into small pieces. Crumple the pieces of newspaper by hand. Ease

gently into the opening of your project for stuffing. Be careful not to use large pieces of newspaper

or the project will tear while you are filling it, and may be lumpy in appearance.

Papier-mâché
MIXING THE PASTE

Mix dry wallpaper paste with water, following the instructions on the package. Make 3 cups of liquid paste. Add small amounts of water as needed to keep paste the desired consistency (It should be liquid, but thicker than water). The container holding the liquid paste should have an opening large enough for your hand to scoop out the paste.

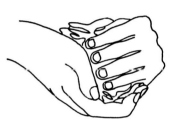

STRIP METHOD

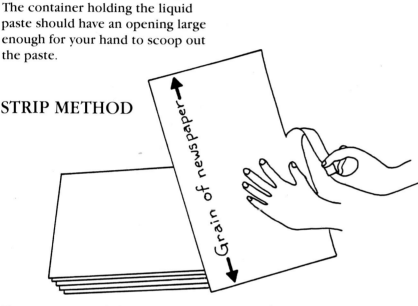

Tear or cut several double sheets of newspaper into 2-in (5-cm) -wide strips as shown. Crumple a

single sheet of newspaper into a tight ball to use as a base. Using

your hands, wipe paste all over the newspaper ball.

Dip the newspaper strips into the paste, coating both sides. Spread the paste with your fingers as shown. Wrap the wet strips around the newspaper ball.

Continue, alternating the direction of the strips. Smooth all the edges down well with paste-covered hands. The ball will grow and become pliable. When pliable, model the ball into a shape for

your project. To add features such as eyes, ears, or nose fasten small balls of crumpled newspaper to the project using newspaper strips covered with paste as you would use tape.

FOR LARGER PROJECTS

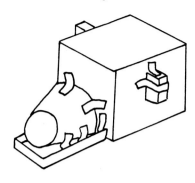
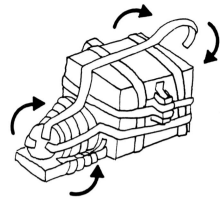

For larger projects, tie, tape, and glue boxes of various sizes onto a base. Note: strips can be placed directly on any project base. Animals and dinosaurs are fun to

make from boxes and papier-mâché. Wrap basic box structure with strip after strip of paste-covered newspaper. Alternate the direction of the strips. Smooth

down the edges with paste using your fingers. Allow to dry. Paint. When thoroughly dry, decorate and shellac.

SLAB METHOD

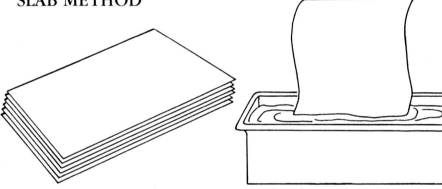
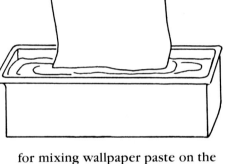
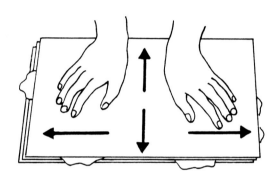

For each slab required for your project, use 6 single sheets of newspaper. Mix 3 cups of liquid wallpaper paste in a shallow, open container. Follow the directions

for mixing wallpaper paste on the package. Dip each single sheet of newspaper into the paste at one time. Lay the sheets one on top of the other, until you have 6 layers.

Smooth the slab with your hands each time you add another layer. Allow excess paste to come out at the sides. Let the slab set for 30 minutes. The layers will adhere to

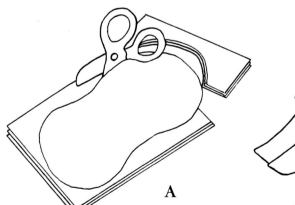

A

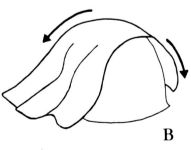

B

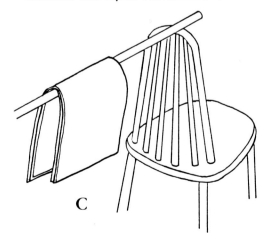

C

each other to make the slab. Depending on your project, the slab may be cut to shape with a sharp scissors (A) when wet or dry. When dry, slabs are smooth

and hard. Or wet slabs may be laid over any mold (B) and allowed to dry in that shape, then trimmed.

Or wet slabs may be hung over a rod suspended between 2 chairs (C) and allowed to dry, then trimmed.

FOR LARGER PROJECTS

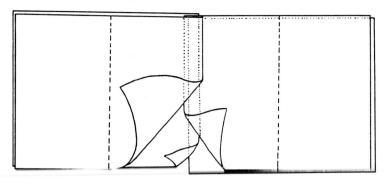

If you require a larger slab, lay the newspaper sheets side by side, overlapping slightly as shown.

Alternate overlapping direction for best results. You will need additional sheets to make the slab 6 layers thick all over.

FOR LIGHTWEIGHT SLABS

Mobiles may require *lightweight slabs* to allow hanging from threads. Use 2 layers of newspapers instead of 6. Follow the same procedure.

PULP METHOD

Fill a one gallon (4 L) ice cream bucket with 2 in (5 cm) squares of newspapers. Cover with warm water. Allow to stand overnight.

To use pulp, add 2 tablespoons of dry wallpaper paste to one cup of pulp. The mixture will keep in a refrigerator for one week only.

One cup pulp is usually sufficient for most projects. Add a few drops of oil of cloves to keep the project fresh and sweet smelling.

Papier-mâché pulp models almost as well as clay. Dry the project quickly in a warm, airy place.

Objects may be sanded when dry. You may paint, varnish, or shellac objects.

When hard and dry, objects become unbreakable.

Newspaper brushes

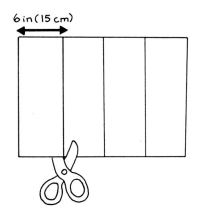

6 in (15 cm)

2 in (5 cm)

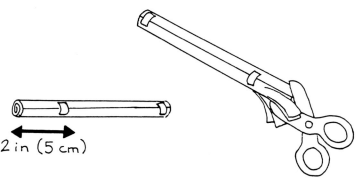

Cut a double sheet of newspaper into 6-in (15-cm) -wide strips. Roll

each strip into a tight tube. Tape at one end. Tape in 2 in (5 cm) from the other end. Make 4 equally spaced 2 in (5 cm) cuts in the untaped end. You will need one

brush for each color you use. Once the paint is allowed to dry on the brush it cannot be used again.

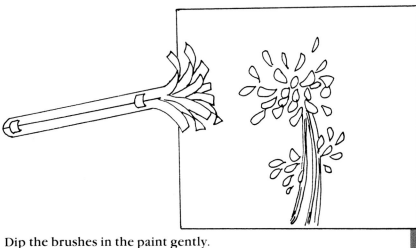

Dip the brushes in the paint gently. These brushes make delicate strokes and can be used to paint flowers, leaves, feathers, hair, fur, or clouds.

Making "Oil" paint

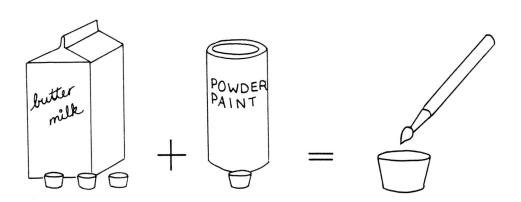

Mix 3 parts buttermilk to 1 part dry poster paint. This resembles oil paint and will not rub off easily.

EASY DOES IT

Cut-out borders

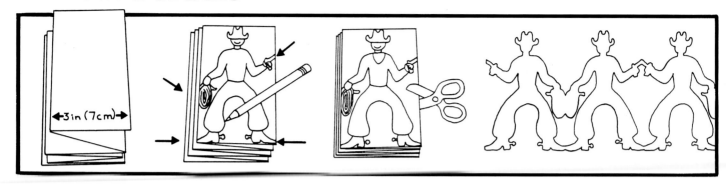

Cut a strip the length of a double sheet of newspaper. Make the strip as wide as you wish the finished panel figures to be tall. Accordion pleat the strip (p 9), starting at one end, using 3 in (7 cm) folds. Draw a design on the top panel as shown. Be sure parts of the design extend over the folds on the 2 sides (see arrows). Carefully cut out the pattern through all thicknesses, but do not cut through the folds where the design touches the sides. Open out the border. Draw in details and paint or color as desired.

Fans

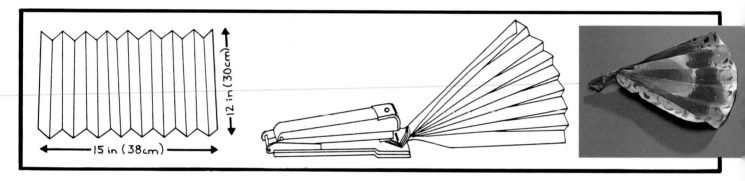

Cut a strip of newspaper 15 in (38 cm) long and 12 in (30 cm) wide. Paint if desired and allow to dry. Make accordion pleating (p 9) from shorter end. Staple one end as shown. Spread out the other end. For decoration, if desired, staple on a ribbon loop and glue a bit of lace along the top edge.

Stars

Fold one sheet of newspaper and draw triangles on the top sheet as shown. Cut out triangles. You will have 2 of each size. Glue the pairs of same-sized triangles together. Then glue 3, 4, or 5 triangles one on top of the other with points sticking in different directions to make a star. Paint the stars different colors. Brush glue on both sides of the stars and sprinkle with glitter. Suspend the star from a thread glued to the star.

Turkeys

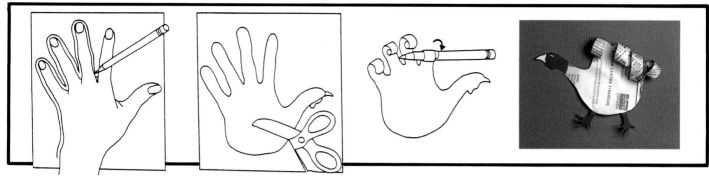

Place the child's hand on a sheet of newspaper. Trace an outline. On the thumb outline draw a point for the beak and a wavy line for the wattle as shown. Cut out the

hand shape. Curl the newspaper fingers around a pencil. This represents the curled tail feathers. Paint the thumb red for the turkey

head. Draw 2 turkey feet on newspaper. Cut out and glue to the turkey body.

Baskets

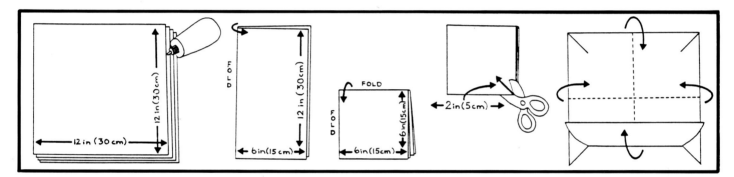

Cut 4 squares of newspaper 12 in by 12 in (30 cm by 30 cm). Glue all 4 sheets together, one on top of the next. Allow to dry. Fold the square exactly in half. Fold in half again making a small square. On

one of the unfolded edges draw a line 2 in (5 cm) from the unfolded corner as shown. Cut along this line. (A longer cut will make a smaller, deeper basket.) Spread the square flat. Fold up each side to the

top of the cut line. Fold each corner piece over the other, and glue together.

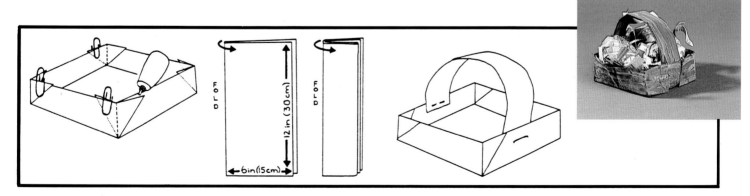

Hold in place with paper clips or clothespins until dry. Make a handle by folding a 12 in by 12 in (30 cm by 30 cm) square of newspaper in half, then fold again

lengthwise. Attach one end of the handle to one side of the basket with glue or a staple. Bend the newspaper handle over the basket and attach to the other side. Fill

the basket with shredded newspaper for straw. Cut out eggs from colored paper for an Easter basket.

Picture frame

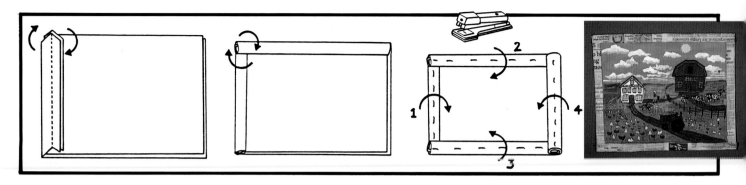

Spread out one double sheet of newspaper, and place another double sheet on top of it. Make a folded border along each edge by folding each edge over twice using

1 in (2 cm) folds. Staple the corners and down each side to make the edges secure. This makes a frame around the center section. In center section paint a picture

or glue on drawings, cutouts, snapshots, or create a collage. These will be the "picture" inside the newspaper frame.

Bowls

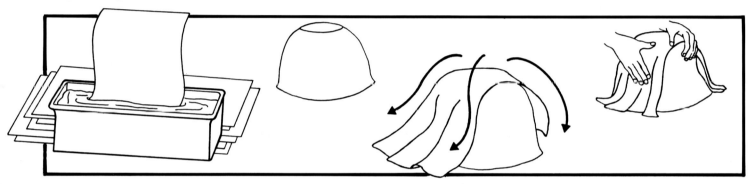

Choose a bowl for a pattern and place the bowl upside down on a flat surface. Use 8 single sheets of newspaper. Place each sheet, as

you use it, in a large container of warm water. Make sure each sheet is completely wet before using. Lay one sheet of wet newspaper over the bowl, and press down

firmly along the edges of the bowl. Lay another sheet of wet newspaper over the bowl, alternating the direction from the first sheet.

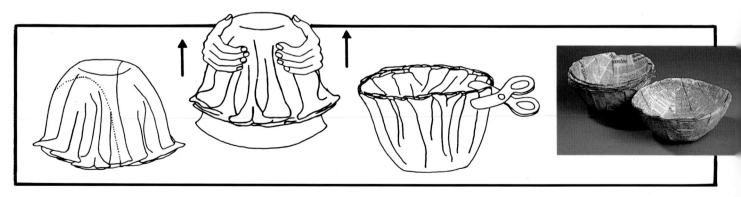

Press down firmly and smooth out the edges. Repeat this procedure until the 8 sheets of wet newspaper have been used, making sure

to alternate the direction of each layer. Allow to dry. The newspaper bowl will lift off when dry. Trim the edges with scissors.

Paint and decorate as desired.

Beads, earrings, bracelets

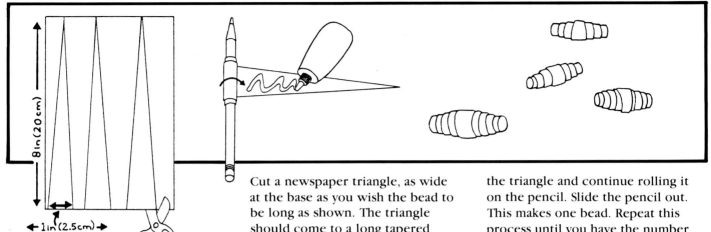

Cut a newspaper triangle, as wide at the base as you wish the bead to be long as shown. The triangle should come to a long tapered point, 8 times as long as the width of the base. Wrap the base of the triangle around a pencil once. Brush glue over the remainder of the triangle and continue rolling it on the pencil. Slide the pencil out. This makes one bead. Repeat this process until you have the number of beads you require. Allow the beads to dry. You may paint the beads if you wish. Or use color comics for interesting patterns.

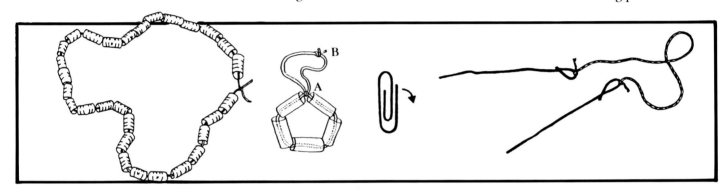

Thread a string through the holes and tie the ends for a necklace. Thread a shorter string for a bracelet. For earrings, thread 5 beads on the middle of a string. Tie a knot at the ends of the beads A and another knot in the ends of the string B, leaving a loop to slip over the ear as shown. For fancy threading, make a "needle" threader by straightening 2 paper clips until each has only one hook left. Use a long piece of string and tie each end to a needle hook as shown.

To make a fancy necklace

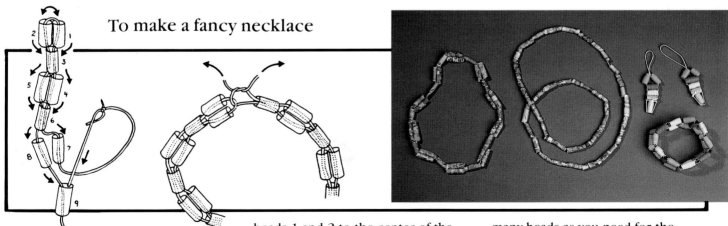

Tie a string 6 ft (2 m) long to your "needle" threader. Thread one needle through 2 beads and slide beads 1 and 2 to the center of the string as shown. Thread one needle through bead 3 and the other needle through the same bead. Repeat the pattern as shown, using as many beads as you need for the desired length. After the last bead, tie the ends together, then tie to the string between beads 1 and 2. Remove hooks and cut off excess string.

STUFF IT

Kid clones

Place 2 double sheets of newspaper, short end to short end as shown. Tape together. Cover with 2 other double sheets of newspaper taped together. Glue the sheets together. Repeat to make another identical large sheet. Allow these sheets to dry. Place one large sheet on top of the other and have the child lie on the sheets as shown. Trace around the child's shape. Cut out very care-

fully through both layers. Glue and staple the edges of the figure together leaving 3 or 4 small openings. When dry, stuff the figure with crumpled newspaper (p 11). Glue the openings shut. Paint the likeness of the child on the front of the shape.

Heart pillow

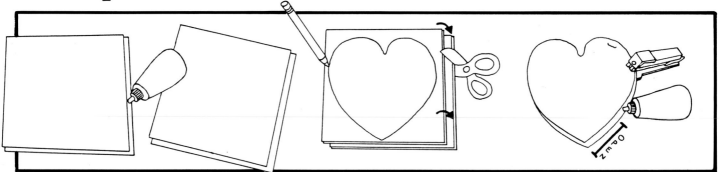

Glue 2 single sheets of newspaper, one on top of the other. Glue 2 *other* single sheets of newspaper together, one on top of the other.

Allow to dry. Place these sheets one on top of the other, as shown. Draw a heart shape. Cut out through both sheets.

Glue heart shapes together around the edges leaving a small opening. (You may wish to staple edges at a few places to provide stability.)

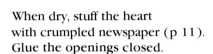

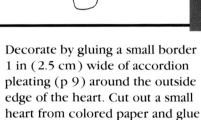

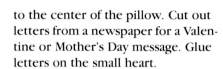

When dry, stuff the heart with crumpled newspaper (p 11). Glue the openings closed.

Decorate by gluing a small border 1 in (2.5 cm) wide of accordion pleating (p 9) around the outside edge of the heart. Cut out a small heart from colored paper and glue

to the center of the pillow. Cut out letters from a newspaper for a Valentine or Mother's Day message. Glue letters on the small heart.

Fish

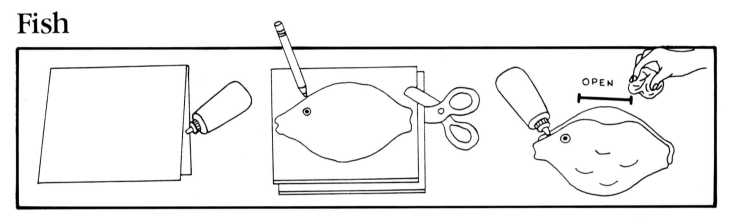

Fold a single sheet of newspaper in half. Glue the halves together. Repeat with another single sheet. Allow to dry. Place one folded sheet

on top of the other. Draw a fish shape. Cut out. Glue the sides of the fish together leaving a small opening.

When dry, stuff the fish with crumpled newspaper (p 11). Glue the opening shut. Allow to dry. Paint on scales, eyes, and mouth.

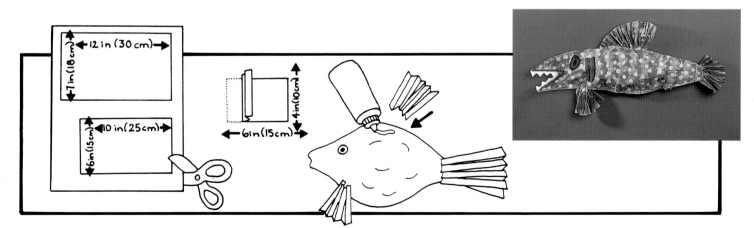

To make fins, from another sheet of newspaper cut out one piece 6 in by 10 in (15 cm by 25 cm) for the top fin, and another piece 6 in by 4 in (15 cm by 10 cm) for the bottom fin. Accordion pleat both

fins (p 9). For the tail, cut out another piece of newspaper 7 in by 12 in (18 cm by 30 cm). Accordion pleat (p 9). Paint fins and tail and glue to fish.

Turtle

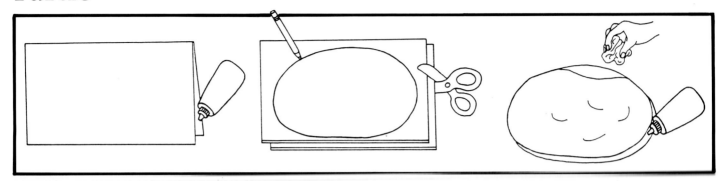

Fold a double sheet of newspaper along the crease. Glue together. Repeat with another double sheet of newspaper. Allow to dry. Place

the sheets one on top of the other and draw an oval outline for the turtle shell on the top sheet. Cut out through both sheets. Glue the

edges together leaving a small opening. When dry, stuff with crumpled newspaper (p 11). Glue the opening closed.

Fold and glue together another double sheet of newspaper. When dry, fold in half. Draw 4 feet, a head, and a tail on the top half. Cut

out through both halves. You will need only one tail. Glue the edges of the feet and the head together leaving small openings as shown. Stuff with small pieces of crumpled

newspaper. Glue the openings closed. When dry, glue the 4 feet, the tail, and the head to the edges of the turtle body as shown. Paint.

Cow that jumped over the moon

Place 2 double sheets of newspaper, one on top of the other. Glue together. Repeat with 2 more sheets. When dry, place one prepared sheet on top of the

other. Draw a cow and moon on the top sheet (or any favorite nursery rhyme theme). Cut out through both sheets. Glue the edges of the cutouts together leav-

ing a small opening. When dry, stuff the cutout with crumpled newspaper (p 11). Glue the opening shut. Paint to resemble a cow and moon.

Octopus

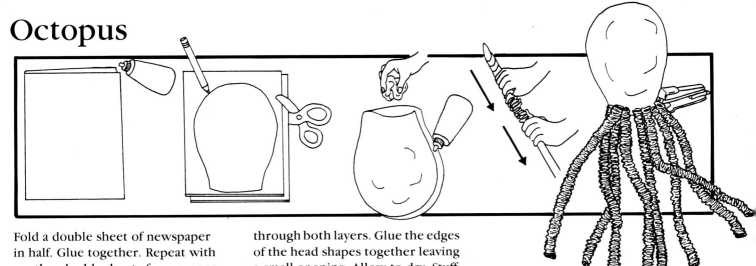

Fold a double sheet of newspaper in half. Glue together. Repeat with another double sheet of newspaper. Allow these to dry. Place one sheet on top of the other. Draw the head of an octopus as shown. Cut out

through both layers. Glue the edges of the head shapes together leaving a small opening. Allow to dry. Stuff the head shape with crumpled newspaper (p 11). Glue the opening closed.

Make 8 crushed newspaper tubes (p 10) for octopus arms. Using glue and staples, attach each arm firmly to the neck part of the head shape as shown.

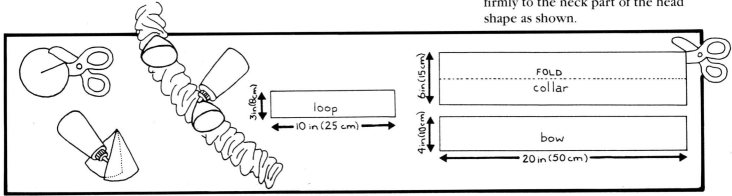

Make suction cups for the octopus arms, using colored construction paper. Draw circles on the paper about 3 in (7 cm) in diameter. Cut out, then make a cut from the outer edge to the center of each circle

as shown. Overlap the cut edges and fold into cup-shaped cones. Glue. Make 5 cups for each arm. Glue the cups to the octopus arms. Paint a friendly face on the octopus head.

Make a collar and bow tie to place over neck and arm joins. For the collar, cut a strip of colored construction paper 6 in by 20 in (15 cm by 50 cm). Fold in half lengthwise and

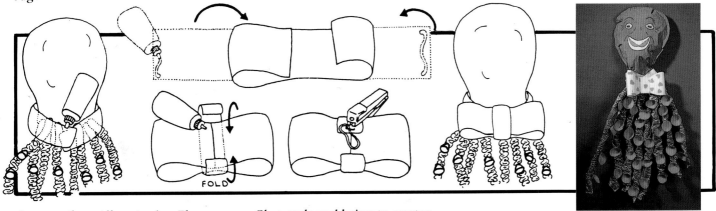

glue together. Allow to dry. Place around neck of octopus, overlap ends at the front, and glue as shown. Make a bow tie. Cut a strip of construction paper 4 in by 20 in (10 cm by 50 cm) for the bow.

Glue ends and bring to center. Press down to form a bow. To make the center loop, cut out another piece of construction paper 3 in by 10 in (7 cm by 25 cm). Fold around center of bow.

Glue ends down at back as shown. Staple a large elastic band to the back of the bow as shown. Stretch the band over the head of the octopus to hold tie in place.

Snowman and Snowlady

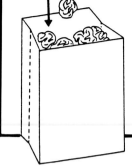 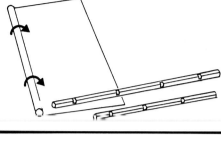 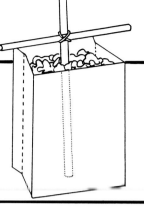 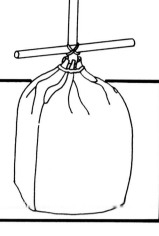

Stuff a large brown paper bag with crushed newspaper for the body of the snowman. Make a tightly rolled newspaper tube the length of a single sheet of newspaper (p 8)

for the "spine," and place it in the center of the bag surrounded by crushed newspaper as shown. Allow the tube to stick up through the opening of the bag about 3 in (7 cm). Make another newspaper

tube the length of a single sheet of newspaper (p 8) and lash it with string to the first tube above the top of the bag. Draw top edges of the paper bag together and tape as shown.

 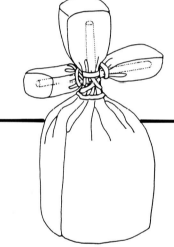

Fill 3 smaller brown paper bags with crushed newspaper for the head and arms. Place the head bag down over the vertical newspaper tube to meet the horizontal tube and tape in place. Place one arm bag over each end of the horizontal tube and tape as shown. For the snowlady, make a second figure by repeating the entire procedure.

Decorate the snowman with a carrot nose. Make the carrot using the cone technique (p 9). Make the carrot about 5 in (12 cm) long and attach by making 3 cuts in the base of the cone and gluing the tabs to the face. Hold in place with tape until glue dries. Remove tape.

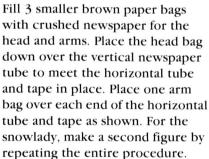 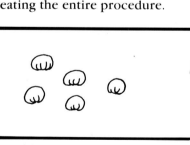 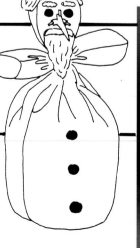

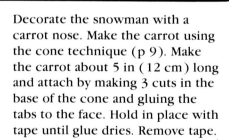

Use the button technique (p 11) for the eyes and buttons. Paint. Glue in place. Tape until glue dries. Remove tape. Paint all over with white strokes for snow. Glue on a small piece of cotton batting for the beard and a longer strip of cotton batting for the hair and 2 short strips for the eyebrows.

28

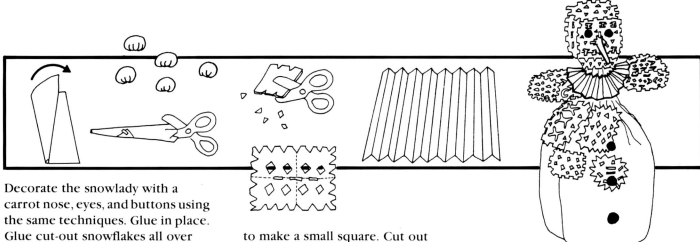

Decorate the snowlady with a carrot nose, eyes, and buttons using the same techniques. Glue in place. Glue cut-out snowflakes all over the body and head. Make the snowflakes from a 6 in by 6 in (15 cm by 15 cm) square of white paper. Fold in half and fold in half again to make a small square. Cut out bits of paper around the edges. Unfold to reveal a snowflake pattern. Make many of these. Glue onto the body. Make a collar from colored construction paper 5 in by 24 in (12 cm by 60 cm). Accordion pleat (p 9). Place around snowlady's neck and glue in place.

Hobby horse

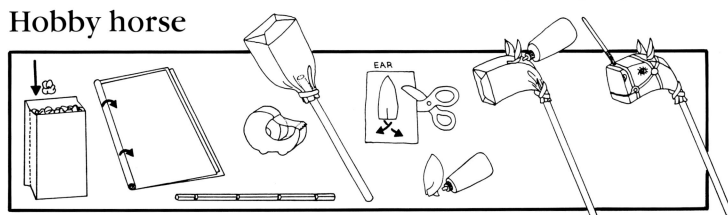

To make the horse's head, stuff a small brown paper bag with crumpled newspaper (p 11). To make the hobby horse stick, roll 3 double sheets of newspaper placed one on top of the other to make a strong tube (p 8). Tape. Place the bag over the end of the stick. Draw the ends of the bag together and tape to the stick. Bend the bag head over gently. Draw an ear shape as shown on a piece of newspaper. Make 2. Cut out. Make a cut 1 in (2.5 cm) deep in the bottom of each ear. Twist the cut pieces one over the other as shown and glue together. Then glue to the head as shown. Paint the ears. Paint on eyes, nostrils, and a bridle. Add circles of glitter or other decoration of your choice.

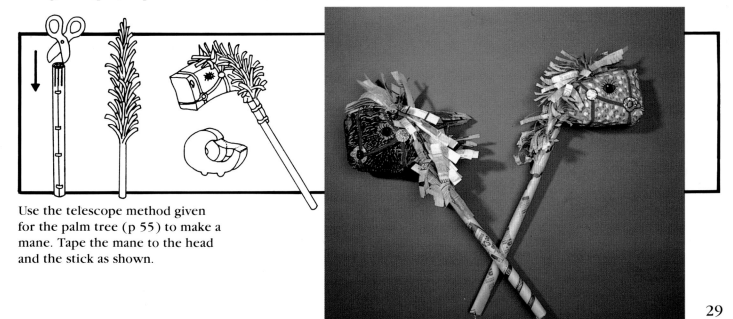

Use the telescope method given for the palm tree (p 55) to make a mane. Tape the mane to the head and the stick as shown.

PUPPETS & PARTIES

Piñata

To make the body of the piñata figure, blow up a balloon. Tie end. Tear or cut 2 in (5 cm) strips from double sheets of newspaper as shown.

Prepare wallpaper paste (p 12). Dip newspaper strips into paste and cover the balloon alternating the direction of the strips as

you cover. Wrap a strong piece of string around the balloon between the layers of newspaper strips as shown. Tie a knot. Allow 3 ft (1

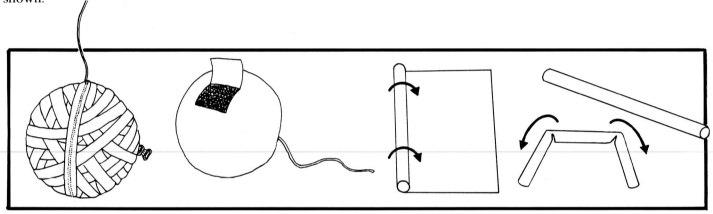

m) of string to stick out at the top for hanging the piñata. Do not make the newspaper layers too thick or the children will not be able to break the piñata.
When the body of the piñata is dry, cut a 2-in (5-cm) -square opening

at the bottom leaving one uncut side as shown. Break the balloon and remove it, leaving a hollow to fill with treats. Fill with wrapped candies or small wrapped gifts. Tape the opening closed.

To make legs for the figure, make 2 newspaper tubes (p 8) by rolling from the short end of 2 single sheets of newspaper. Tape closed. Fold each tube into thirds. Attach

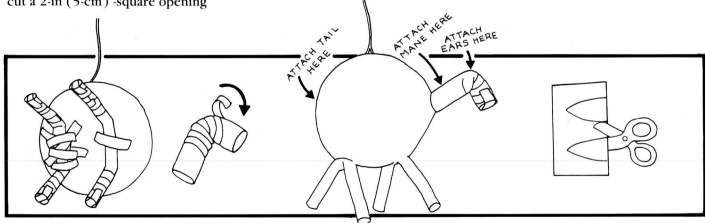

the middle third to the bottom of the body with newspaper strips dipped in wallpaper paste. Allow to dry.

Make a larger newspaper tube for the head and neck. Bend the tube in the middle. Cover with newspaper strips dipped in wallpaper paste. Attach one end to one side

of the body with more newspaper strips dipped in paste. Allow to dry. Draw 2 triangles on newspaper and cut out for the ears. Attach the ears to the head using newspaper strips dipped in wallpaper paste.

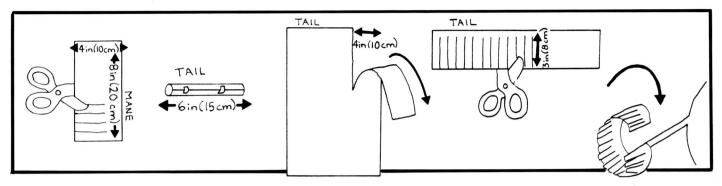

For a mane, cut a piece of newspaper 4 in (10 cm) wide by 8 in (20 cm) long. Make cuts along one side for a fringe. Glue to neck and head of the piñata figure as shown below.

For a tail, make a thin newspaper tube by rolling a piece of newspaper 6 in (15 cm) wide and 15 in (90 cm) long. Roll from short end. Attach the thin tube to the back end of the balloon shape with

newspaper strips dipped in paste. Cut a strip 4 in (10 cm) wide and the length of a single sheet of newspaper. Make cuts 3 in (7.5 cm) deep along one side to make a fringe. Wrap the uncut side of the fringe around the tail tube. Glue in place. Paint and decorate.

Tie the loose string end to a tree branch so the piñata hangs freely. Children (usually blindfolded) hit the piñata with sticks to release the gifts.

Party surprise ball

Select a small gift for each child attending the party. Cut a number of long strips of newspaper 1 in (2.5 cm) wide. Tape the end of the first strip of newspaper to the largest gift. Wrap around gift. Tape

another strip of newspaper to the end of the first strip and continue to wrap the gift. When the first gift is covered with newspaper add a second gift. Continue in this way until all the gifts are covered.

Children discover their gifts by sitting in a circle and passing the surprise ball around the circle, unwinding the ball as it is passed, until each child has received a gift.

Ring toss game

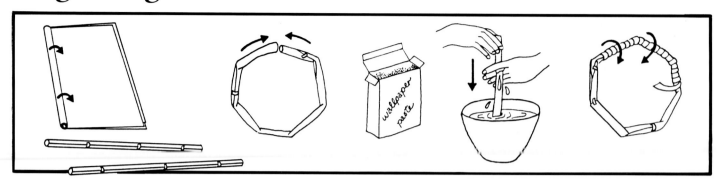

Place 2 double sheets of newspaper one on top of the other. Beginning at the longer end, roll into a tube. Make 3 of these tubes, one for each ring.

To make the rings, bend each tube into a circle as shown and slip one end of the tube into the other end. Tape to secure each circle. Tear

single sheets of newspaper into 1-in (2.5-cm) -wide strips. Dip strips in wallpaper paste and wrap around the rings until they are well covered. Allow to dry. Paint

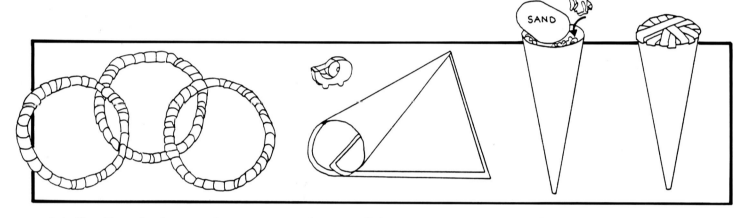

and shellac. To make the peg, place 2 double sheets of newspaper one on top of the other and roll into a cone (p 9). Tape to secure the

cone shape. Stuff the cone with crumpled newspaper (p 11). Stuff the wide end of the cone with a sandbag or rocks to give the base

weight. Cover the opening with paste-covered newspaper strips. Layer in alternating directions to make a flat base. Tear single sheets

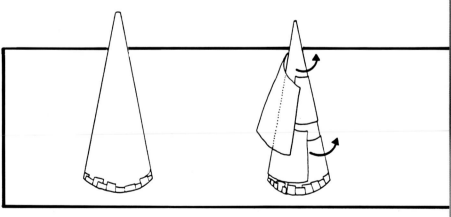

of newspaper into 5-in (12-cm) -wide strips and dip them in wallpaper paste. Wrap the cone with 3 layers of these newspaper strips.

Paint and shellac. Stand cone on base. Toss rings over the cone to play the game.

Pumpkin money bank

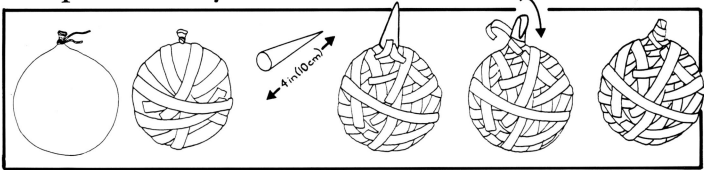

Blow up a balloon. Tie the end. Cover with 2 or 3 layers of 1-in (2.5-cm)-wide strips of newspaper dipped in wallpaper paste. Flatten bottom slightly. For the pumpkin stem, make a small cone (p 9) about 4 in (10 cm) long. Make 3 cuts in the base of the cone, fold back, and attach to the balloon shape over the tied end, using newspaper strips dipped in wallpaper paste. Fold over the pointed end of the cone and cover with newspaper strips dipped in wallpaper paste. Make enough layers until the stem is the desired

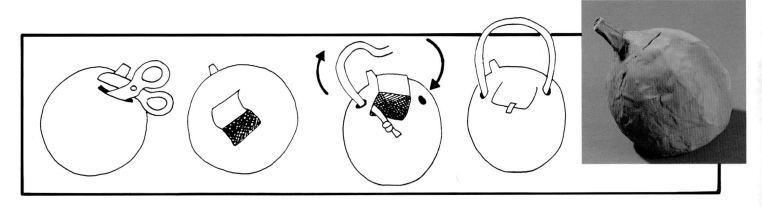

thickness. Allow to dry. Paint. Cut a slit in the top of the pumpkin to put the money in the bank. Cut a trap door in the bottom as shown. Remove the popped balloon. Tape the door closed.

For a *trick or treat bag* for Halloween cut the trap door in the top instead of the money slit. Do not cut bottom. Attach carrying handles by cutting a hole on each side of the trap-door opening and threading through strips of plastic bags. Knot the ends of bags inside the pumpkin.

Rattles and maracas

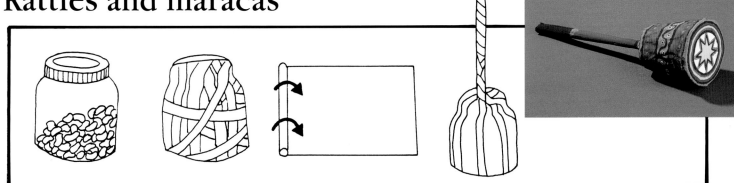

Put a few beans, macaroni, or rice in glass baby food jars. Do not fill jars. Make sure the lids are secure. Wrap the jars with 1-in (2.5 cm)-wide strips of newspaper dipped in wallpaper paste. For the handle, make a tight newspaper roll (p 8) from a single sheet of newspaper. Attach to top end of covered jar with strips of newspaper dipped in wallpaper paste. Allow to dry. Paint and shellac.

Hand puppets

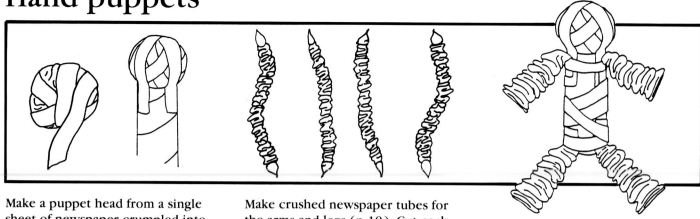

Make a puppet head from a single sheet of newspaper crumpled into a ball. Cover with 1-in (2.5-cm) -wide newspaper strips dipped in wallpaper paste. With a paste-covered newspaper strip, attach the head to the end of a toilet tissue roll as shown.

Make crushed newspaper tubes for the arms and legs (p 10). Cut each arm and leg 5 in (12 cm) long. Attach the crushed tubes to the toilet tissue roll with newspaper strips dipped in paste as shown. Cover the entire toilet tissue roll in this way, leaving the bottom

hole of the toilet tissue roll open to insert fingers to hold the puppet. Make 2 other puppets in the same way.

For the *princess,* make a dress from a newspaper cone (p 9) 7 in (18 cm) long. Tape closed. Cut off the pointed end of the cone so it will fit over the toilet tissue roll as shown. Attach the "dress" with paste-covered newspaper strips.

Cover the entire cone with these strips. Allow to dry. Cut a strip of newspaper as wide as you wish the length of the puppet's hair to be,

and fringe one side (p 10). Glue in place around puppet head for hair. Cut another strip and fringe it for the bangs. Glue in place. Make a crown from a newspaper strip. Wrap around the puppet head and glue. Cut notches to make the crown points as shown.

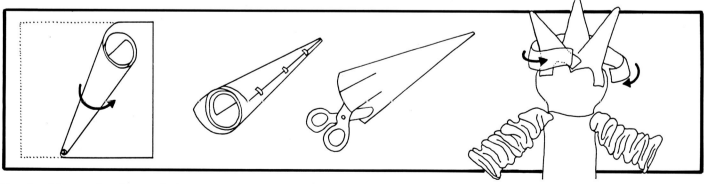

For the *king,* make shorter hair and crown.

For the *jester,* make 3 small newspaper cones 2 in (5 cm) long. Attach to head as shown with newspaper strips dipped in wallpaper paste.

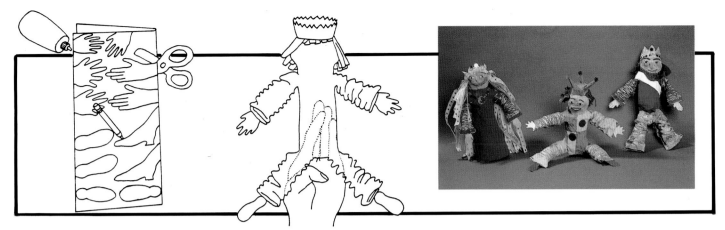

Fold a single sheet of newspaper in half and glue together. Draw 6 hands and 6 feet to fit the size of your puppets. Cut out. Glue to the sleeves and legs of each figure.

When all are assembled, and thoroughly dry, paint and decorate. Place fingers inside puppets to make them participate in a puppet show.

Hollow tree house

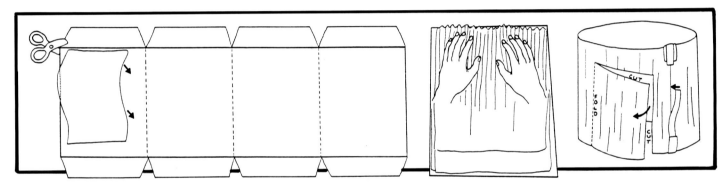

Use a large cardboard box from a refrigerator or mattress container. Open out flat. Trim off ends and discard. Dip single sheets of newspaper into thin wallpaper paste, soaking both sides of newspaper. Lay on top of one side of the cardboard. Smooth sheets out well.

While still wet, place flattened hands on the newspaper sheets and move the hands around gently to create a rippled effect across the entire cardboard surface. Allow to dry. When dry and painted, this rippled surface resembles tree bark.

Stand the project on end and gently bend the cardboard into a circle to form a hollow tree trunk. Tape the ends together. Cover joined edges with strips of newspaper dipped in wallpaper paste. Allow to dry.
Cut a door in the back of the tree house as shown. Cut out a circle

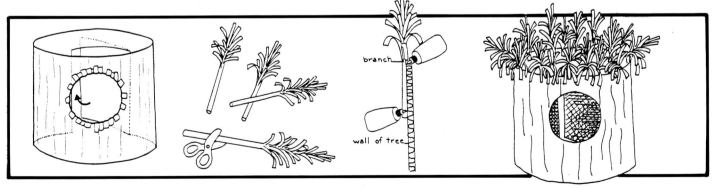

opening in the front. Cover the opening edges with paste-covered newspaper strips. When dry, paint to resemble tree bark.
To make branches and leaves,

make 25 telescoping tube palm trees (p 55). Cut off 12 in (30 cm) from the bottom of the tubes. Spatter with green paint to resemble leaves. Glue and tape the tubes

along the top inside edge of the tree house as shown, leaving the "leaves" sticking out. See photograph on p 31.

37

Marionettes

Marionettes are maneuvered by tube-rods attached to the puppet figures with strings.

Crocodile

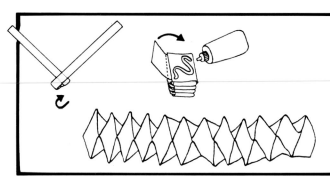

Make one catstair (p 11) 12 in (30 cm) long for the crocodile body. Fold the catstair together and paint *edges only* (see photograph). Fold a single sheet of newspaper in half.

Glue together. When dry, draw and cut out 4 crocodile feet and one crocodile tail as shown. Glue to catstair body. Fold the remaining piece of newspaper in half as

shown. Draw a triangle for the head and mouth using folded side as the base of the triangle. Make the base of the triangle as wide as the catstair width. Cut out. Cut

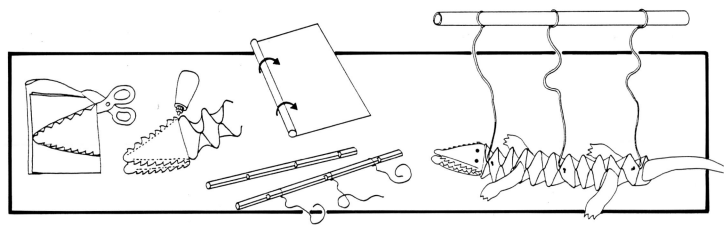

jagged edges along sides of triangle for crocodile teeth. Paint mouth and teeth. Glue the folded edge to the catstair as shown. Make a thin

newspaper tube (p 8) 12 in (30 cm) long. Tie 3 strings around the tube to attach to the crocodile body. Attach strings from the tube-

rod to the crocodile body. Thread string end through darning needle, poke needle through catstair, remove needle, knot end of string.

38

Snake

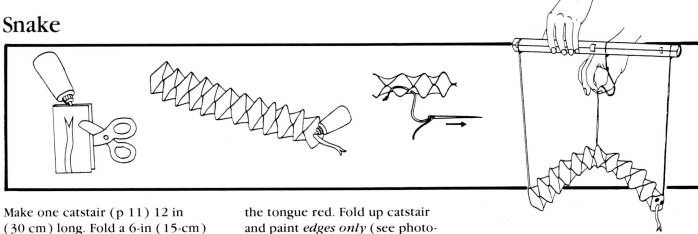

Make one catstair (p 11) 12 in (30 cm) long. Fold a 6-in (15-cm) -square piece of newspaper in half and glue together. When dry, draw a forked tongue and cut out. Glue tongue to one end of the catstair. Paint a snake face on this end. Paint the tongue red. Fold up catstair and paint *edges only* (see photograph). Make a thin newspaper tube (p 8) 12 in (30 cm) long. Tie 3 strings as shown around the tube-rod and attach the strings and the tube-rod to the snake body as shown. Thread free end of string through a darning needle and poke through the snake body. Remove needle and tie a knot in the string end. Repeat for the other 2 strings.

Ostrich

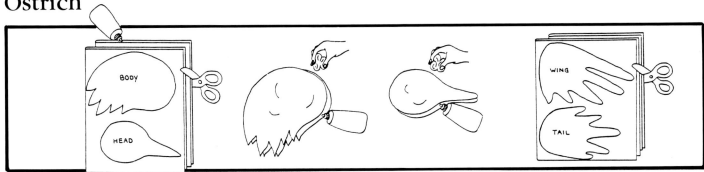

Make 3 catstairs (p 11), each 8 in (20 cm) long for ostrich legs and neck. For the body, head, wings, and tail, glue 2 single sheets of newspaper one on top of the other. Make 4 of these. When dry, place one sheet over another sheet and draw an ostrich body and head as shown. Cut out. Glue body pieces and head pieces together along the edges, leaving an opening. When dry, stuff loosely with torn-up newspaper (p 11). Glue openings closed. Use the remaining 2 sheets for the wings and tail. Place the remaining 2 sheets of newspaper together one on top of the other. Draw a wing and a tail on the top layer. Cut out through both sheets to make 2 wings and 2 tails. Glue one wing on each side of the body and the 2 tails to the back end of the body.

Glue the head to the catstair neck.

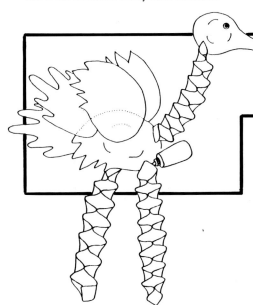

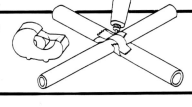

Glue the neck and legs to the body as shown. Paint body, wings, head, and tail. Fold up catstairs and paint *edges only.*

Make 2 tight tube-rods (p 8) for maneuvering. Tape and glue in a cross as shown. Tie 4 strings around rods as shown, and attach the other end of the strings to the head, body, and feet of the ostrich the same as for the crocodile marionette.

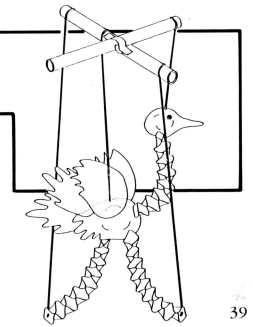

Camel

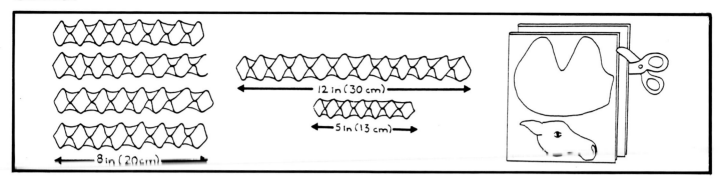

Make 4 catstairs (p 11), each 8 in (20 cm) long for camel legs. Make one catstair 12 in (30 cm) long for a neck. Make one catstair 5 in (12 cm) long for a tail. Set aside.

Glue 2 single sheets of newspaper together. Make 2 of these. When dry, place one on top of the other. On the top layer draw a camel body and head as shown. Cut out.

Glue edges of body pieces and head pieces together as shown leaving small openings in each. When dry, stuff loosely with torn-up newspaper (p 11). Glue

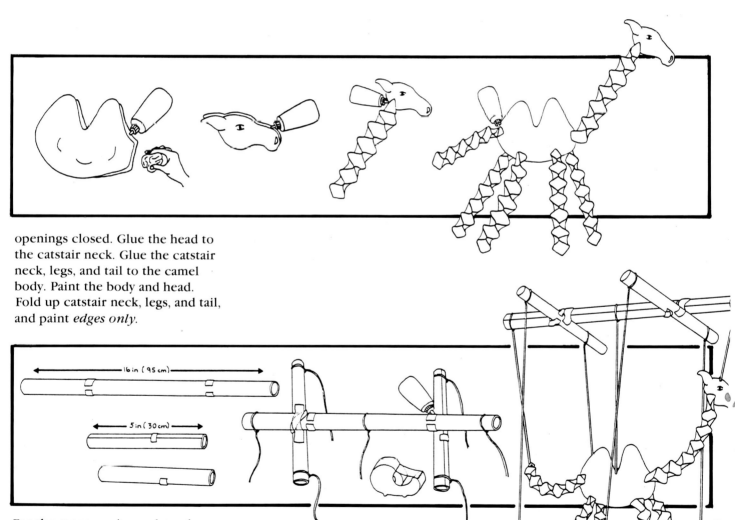

openings closed. Glue the head to the catstair neck. Glue the catstair neck, legs, and tail to the camel body. Paint the body and head. Fold up catstair neck, legs, and tail, and paint *edges only*.

For the maneuvering rods, make one thin rolled newspaper tube (p 8) 16 in (40 cm) long. Make 2 thin tubes each 5 in (12 cm) long. Glue and tape short rods near the ends of the long rod as shown. Tie 7 strings to rods as shown. Attach the strings from the short tubes to the legs. Tie the strings from the long tube to the head, body, and tail of camel as shown. Use same method as for the crocodile.

Puppet theater

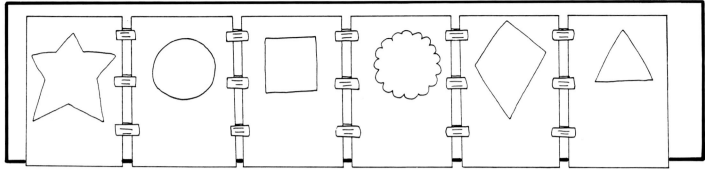

Use 6 sheets of cardboard each 2 ft by 3 ft (60 cm by 90 cm). Cut geometric shapes in each sheet as shown, large enough for the children to put their hands through to maneuver the puppets. Lay the sheets side by side and using a strong tape, join together in 3 places as shown. Tape on both sides. These are the hinges. The sheets can be folded like an accordion for storage.

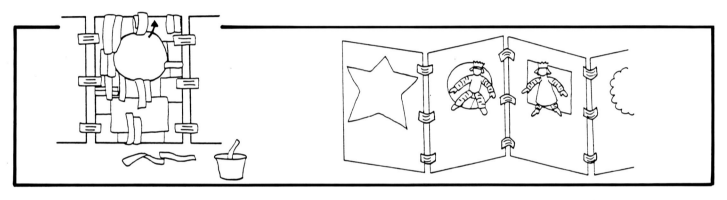

Cover the cardboard with sheets and strips of newspaper dipped in wallpaper paste. Cover both sides and apply newspaper strips around and through the openings. Keep the taped hinges free for folding. When dry, paint and shellac. Stand the project up on the floor or a low table. Six children can perform, each using an opening. Children can make up a story or play and make suitable puppet characters for the parts.

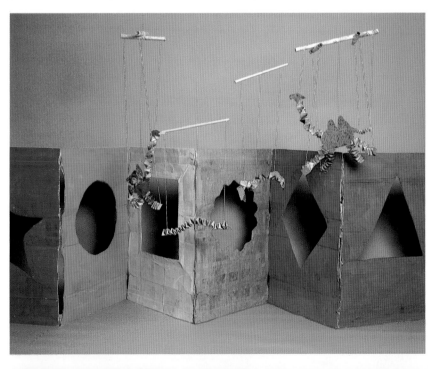

DECORATIONS
&
GIFTS

Bowls or flower pots

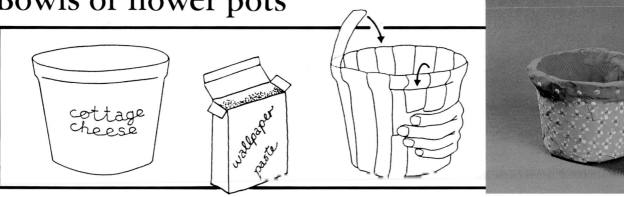

Use an empty cottage cheese plastic carton or similar container. Cover the container inside and out with strips of newspaper dipped in wall-paper paste. Allow to dry. Paint and shellac. This makes a very strong and attractive gift or a handy container for the art room.

Thanksgiving cornucopia

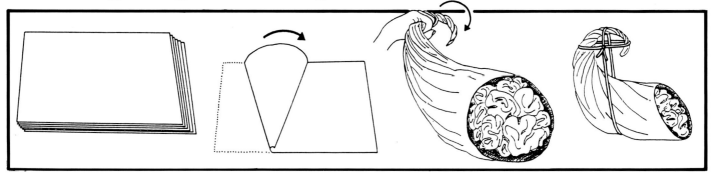

Make a papier-mâché slab (p 13) from 6 single sheets of newspaper. Roll the wet slab, starting three-quarters down the long side, to form a large cone (p 9) for the cornucopia. While wet, twist the end. Tie the end with string and stuff the cone with crumpled news-paper to hold the shape until dry.

Remove string and crumpled newspaper. Paint.

Fill the cornucopia with newspaper fruit and vegetables. Use the button technique (p 11) or crumple news-paper and cover with newspaper strips dipped in wallpaper paste (p 12). While wet, mold to the shape of the desired fruit and vegetables. When dry, paint the fruit and vege-tables. Glue them in the cornucopia.

Hanging planter

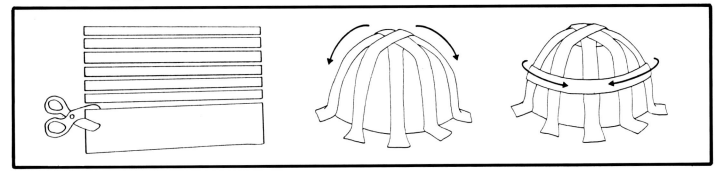

Make a papier-mâché slab (p 13) and cut the wet slab into 8 strips 1 in (2.5 cm) wide. Turn a large plastic bowl upside down to use as

a mold. Cross 6 strips over the bottom of the bowl as shown. Press the strips firmly against the bowl to create a latticed basket. Place

the other 2 strips end to end and overlap. Place them around the side of the bowl as shown. When

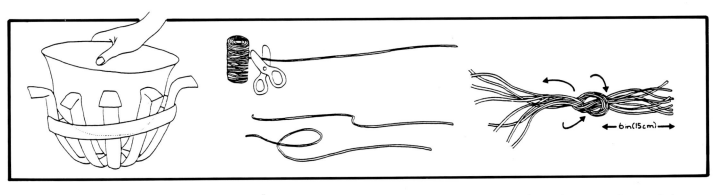

dry, invert and remove the plastic bowl. Paint the hanging basket.

To make the hangar, cut 7 lengths of string, each 3 ft (1 m) long.

Place the strings together and tie a knot about 6 in (15 cm) from one end as shown. Turn the basket

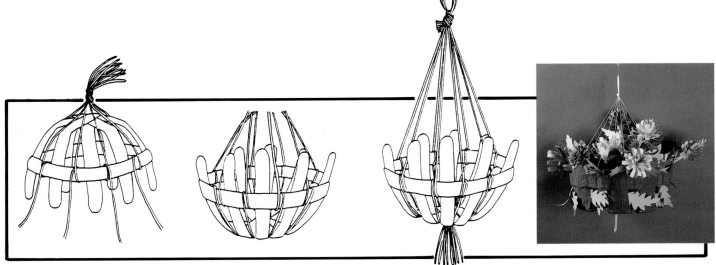

upside down. Place the knot at the center of the basket bottom and put a string between each piece of slab, and wrap the strings once around the basket cross bar as

shown. Turn the basket over. Draw the strings together at the top, and tie, making a loop for hanging. Fill the hanging basket with newspaper flowers (p 59).

Bows

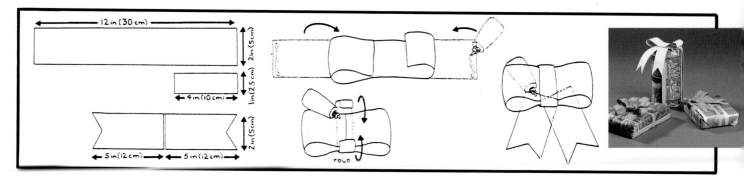

Cut a strip of newspaper 2 in (5 cm) by 12 in (30 cm). Apply glue on each end. Bend each end toward the middle as shown, and press down to hold in place. Cut another

strip 1 in (2.5 cm) by 4 in (10 cm). Wrap around the center of the first strip. Glue in place at the back of the bow as shown. Cut 2 more strips, each 2 in (5 cm) by 5 in

(12 cm). Cut a triangle shape out of one end of each strip. Glue to the back of the bow, pointed ends down, as shown. Paint and decorate with glue sprinkled with glitter. Use to decorate your own gifts!

Christmas bells

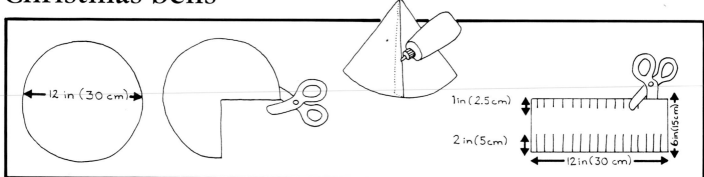

Cut out a circle 12 in (30 cm) in diameter from colored construction paper. (You can also use a double sheet of newspaper folded over and glued together.) Cut a quarter section out of the circle in a pie

shape as shown. Draw the edges of the remaining part of the circle together to form a cone. Overlap edges and glue. Set aside.
Cut out a strip of construction paper (or a double sheet of news-

paper glued together) 6 in (15 cm) wide and 12 in (30 cm) long. Make a row of tabs on each side of the strip as shown — 2-in (5-cm)-deep cuts along one side and 1 in (2.5 cm) cuts along the opposite edge.

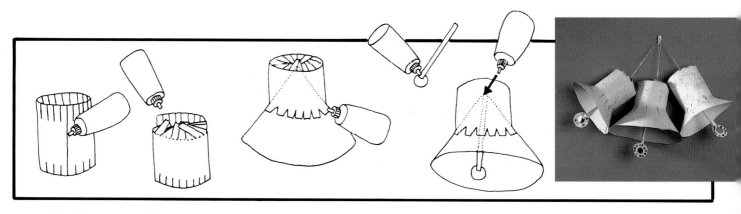

Bring the short ends of the strip together. Overlap and glue. Fold the 2-in (5-cm)-long tabs toward the center of the cylinder, and glue one on top of the other to

form a flat surface. Push the point of the cone into the open end of the cylinder. glue the short tabs to the outside of the cone.
To make a clapper, cut out a narrow

strip of paper or use a pipe cleaner and glue a small circle of paper on the end. Glue the clapper to the inside of the cone/bell. Paint and decorate.

46

Christmas tree

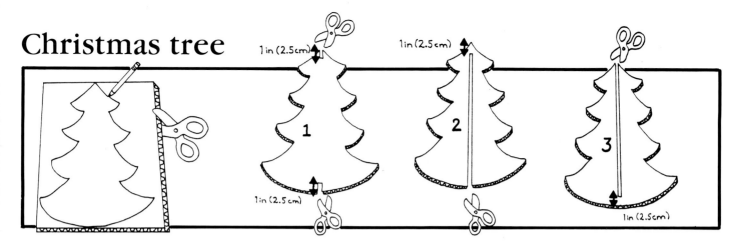

Draw a Christmas tree shape on a large sheet of firm cardboard. Cut out. Use this as a pattern and cut out 2 additional tree shapes from cardboard. Draw a line down the center, from top to bottom, on all the tree shapes.

For the first tree make a 1 in (2.5 cm) cut at the top and bottom of the drawn line as shown. For the second tree cut along the drawn line leaving 1 in (2.5 cm) uncut at the *top* of the tree shape as shown.

For the third tree shape cut along the drawn line leaving 1 in (2.5 cm) uncut at the *bottom* of the tree shape as shown.

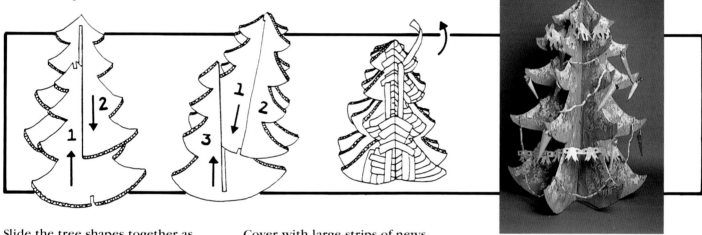

Slide the tree shapes together as shown. The cuts of one tree fit into the other tree shapes vertically. Tape together.

Cover with large strips of newspaper dipped in wallpaper paste. Dry well. Paint green. Decorate.

Decoration ideas

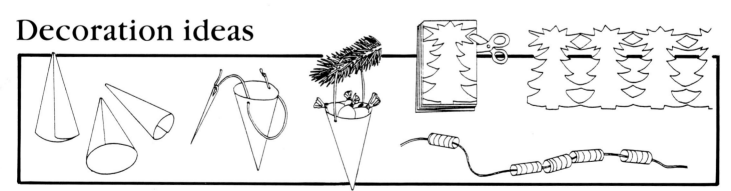

Icicle baskets

Make several newspaper cones (p 9) any size you wish. Paint and decorate with glue sprinkled with glitter, bows, or feathers.
Attach a string handle to the top of the cone for hanging. Poke darning needle and string through cone sides. Knot ends as shown. Larger cones can be filled with candy or flowers to hang on the Christmas tree. Smaller cones can be hung on the tree as icicle decorations.

Christmas tree borders

Make cut-out borders (p 18). Use Christmas themes as your pattern. Drape on tree.

Bead strings

Make newspaper beads (p 21). Thread the beads on a long string to drape on the tree.

47

Christmas wreath

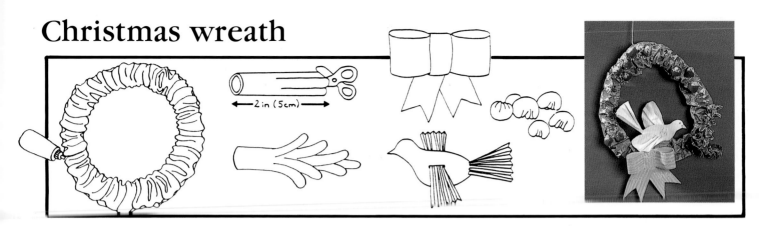

Make one crushed newspaper tube from a double sheet of newspaper (p 10). Glue the ends together to form a circle as shown.
To make a pine cone, cut a piece of newspaper 2 in (5 cm) wide and 6 in (15 cm) long. Roll into a

tube and tape. Make 1 in (2.5 cm) cuts at one end. Pull up center of tube. (See telescope palm tree technique, p. 55.) Make 3 of these. Glue these to the wreath. Make a paper bow (p 46). Attach to the wreath with glue or string. Make a

dove using the hummingbird technique (p 69). Attach to the wreath with glue or string. Make holly berries using the button technique (p 11). Glue to the wreath. Dry thoroughly. Paint. Tie a string around the wreath at the top and leave a loop for hanging.

Christmas yule log

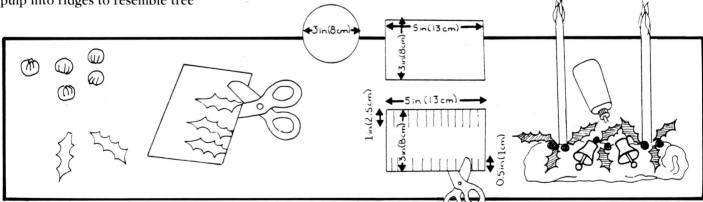

Cover a long cardboard tube (from waxed paper or aluminum foil) with papier-mâché pulp (p 14). Use the fingers to push the pulp into ridges to resemble tree

bark. Add extra papier-mâché pulp to the underside so that the log lies flat without rolling. Allow to dry. Paint brown.

Make 2 candles (p 49). Glue these upright on the top of the log, one near each end.
Make several holly berries using

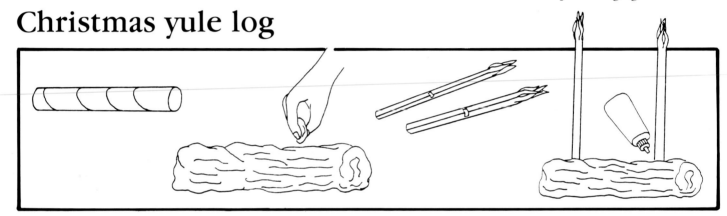

the button technique (p 11). Allow to dry. Paint red.
Cut out holly leaves from green paper. Glue these on the log with the red berries. If desired, add

small bells. Use the Christmas bell technique (p 46), but make the circles for the bell 3 in (8 cm) in diameter and the long strip 3 in (8 cm) wide and 5 in (13 cm) long.

Make 1 in (2.5 cm) cuts down one side of the strip and 0.5 in (1 cm) cuts down the other. Proceed as instructed for bells (p 46). Glue to the yule log. See photograph on p 43.

Candle and Candleholder

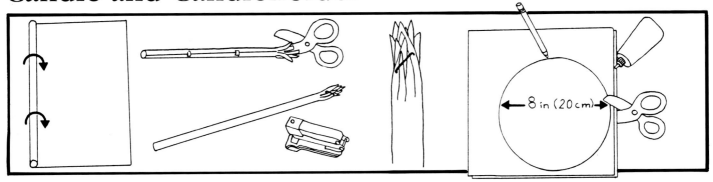

Make the candle by rolling a single sheet of newspaper starting at the short end. To make the flame, make 4 cuts with scissors in one end of the rolled tube (p 8), and

staple the cut ends together into a point. Paint the flame yellow and orange. Paint remainder of candle bright white.

Make the candleholder by gluing together 2 single sheets of newspaper. Draw an 8-in (20-cm) -diameter circle as shown. Cut out.

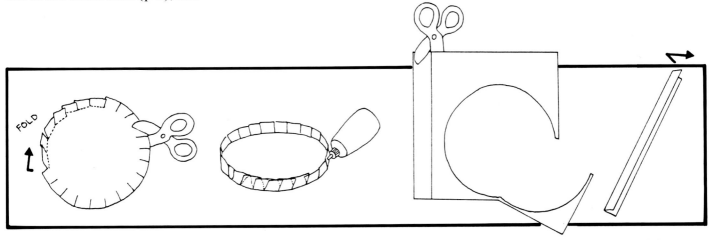

Make 1-in (2.5-cm) -deep cuts all around the outside of the circle as shown.

Fold the cut tabs up. Where the edges overlap, glue the tabs together to make a shallow dish.

From the same newspaper slab cut a strip 3 in (7.5 cm) wide and the length of the newspaper. Fold in half lengthwise. Roll into a cylinder

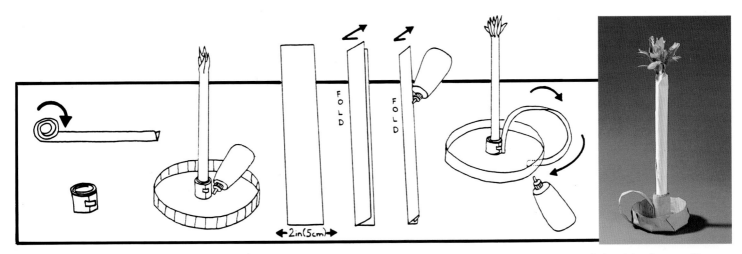

that will fit on the outside bottom of the candle. Tape the end of the cylinder. Place the candle end in the cylinder as shown. Glue the cylinder to the center of the dish.

Cut another strip 2 in (5 cm) wide from the remaining glued newspaper sheets. Fold over lengthwise and fold again. Glue together. Glue one end of the long strip to the cylinder as shown, placing the strip

pointing upwards beside the candle. Tape until glue dries. Curl the free end around and under the dish for the handle. Glue and tape to dish bottom, as shown. Paint when dry.

49

Flower vase

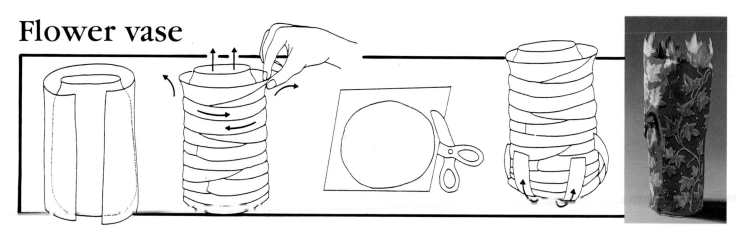

Wrap a wet papier-mâché slab (p 13) around a tall plastic jar. Ends should overlap slightly. Cut off excess slab. Cover the slab with newspaper strips dipped in paste. Turn the top edge of the slab outward so the jar inside can be removed easily when the project is finished. From another papier-mâché slab, cut a circle the size of the bottom of the jar. Fasten it to the bottom of the jar with news-paper strips dipped in wallpaper paste. When dry, remove the plastic container.

Paint the vase and decorate as you wish. If you leave the plastic container in place, the vase can hold water for real flowers.

Cuff link tray or stamp holder

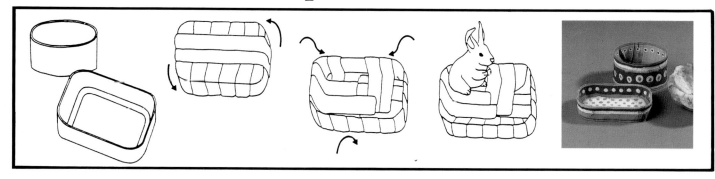

Use a sardine can for a stamp holder or a cough-candy tin for a cuff link tray. Be sure the lids have no sharp edges. Cover the outside of the container with strips of newspaper dipped in wallpaper paste. Cover the inside of the container in the same way. When the papier-mâché is wet, you may wish to decorate the outside with stones, sand, or bits of driftwood. When the papier-mâché is dry, paint and shellac.

Make a small papier-mâché animal using the pulp method (p 14) to sit in the corner of the tray. Allow to dry. Paint and decorate.

Stone sculpture

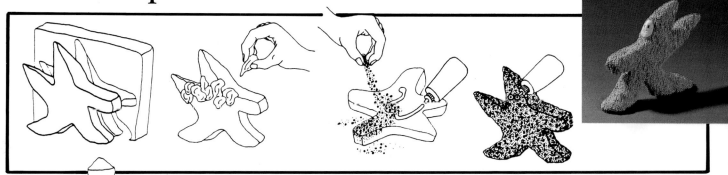

Cut desired shape from a piece of styrofoam. Using the papier-mâché pulp method (p 14), cover the figure completely, molding the shape as you go. Be sure to keep the base flat so the object will stand. When dry, apply glue all over the figure. Sprinkle with sand until the figure is nicely coated. Allow to dry. Glue on buttons or beads for the eyes.

Mobile

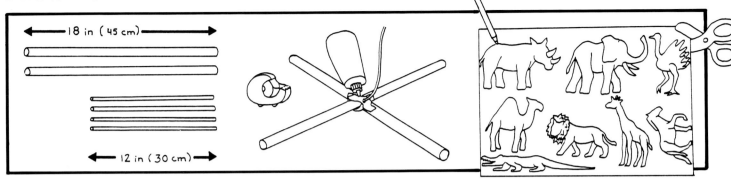

Make 2 newspaper tubes (p 8) each 18 in (45 cm) long. Make 4 slim newspaper tubes 12 in (30 cm) long. Glue the loose ends closed. Tie a string around the center of one large tube to hang the mobile. Cross the larger tubes placing the tube with the string on top and secure with glue and tape.

Make a 2-sheet papier-mâché slab (p 13). Allow to dry. Draw and cut out 8 shapes (such as animals). Paint both sides of each figure.

Glue a 12 in (30 cm) string to the top of each shape. Attach the other end of the string to an end of one of the slim tubes as shown.

Bend the slim tubes over the ends of the large tubes as shown. Glue and tape in place. Mobile is ready for hanging.

Flowers, stems, and leaves

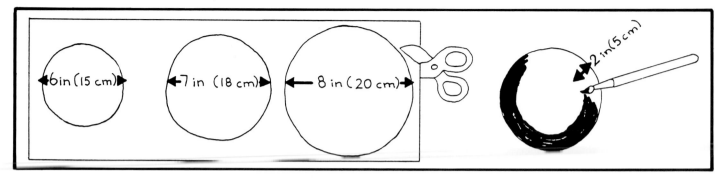

Cut 3 newspaper circles, one each of the following: 6 in (15 cm), 7 in (18 cm), and 8 in (20 cm) in diameter. Paint one side of each

circle completely. Turn over. Paint the edges of each circle in 2 in (5 cm) from the edge as shown.

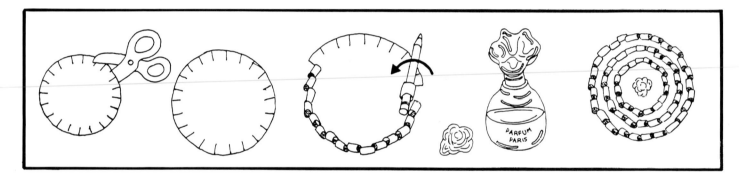

When dry, fringe all around each circle edge by making 1 in (2.5 cm) cuts. Place the completely painted side up and curl each fringe around a

pencil towards the center of the circle as shown. Glue the circles one inside the other. Glue a cotton

ball sprinkled with perfume in the center.

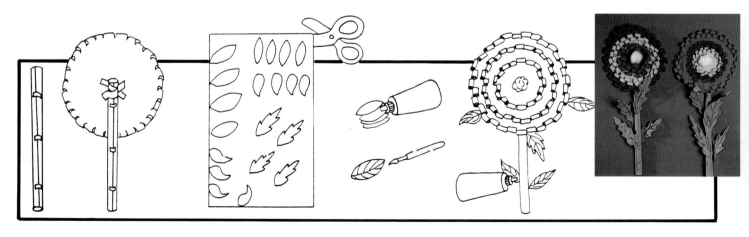

Make the stem by rolling a single sheet of newspaper into a tube (p 8). Tape or glue closed. Cut in lengths to suit the size of the flower. Paint green. Glue or tape to the flower.

Cut out leaf shapes from a single sheet of newspaper. Make 4 of each shape. Glue same shapes, one on top of the other, to make a strong leaf. Paint green. Draw on vein lines

while the paint is wet. Leaves may be shaped to bend around the stem while they are wet. Glue in place around the stems or under the flowers.

Palm trees

Spread out 3 double sheets of newspaper, short end to short end. Overlap the ends 2 in (5 cm) as

shown. Roll tightly from one short end, feeding each sheet into the roll as you come to it. Tape closed.

Make 6 cuts 6 in (15 cm) long in one end of the tube as shown. Take

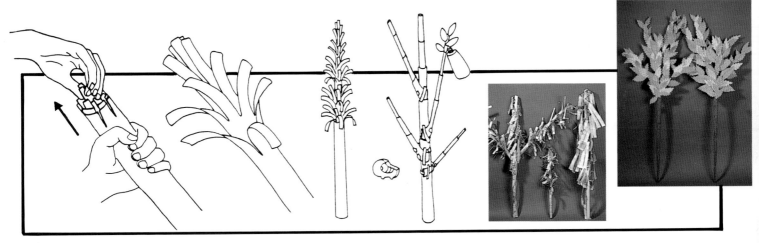

hold of the fringe in the center of the tube at the cut end and carefully pull to elongate the tube, which will pull out like a telescope (p 9). When pulled out, the cut pieces will

hang down giving the effect of a palm tree.
If you wish another kind of tree do not make the cuts in the end. Instead, pull out the telescope for the tree

trunk. Make smaller telescopes using only one double sheet of newspaper for the branches. Tape the branches to the tree trunk. Paint. Attach leaves if desired. Use this method for pine cones as well. See p 48.

Campfire and logs

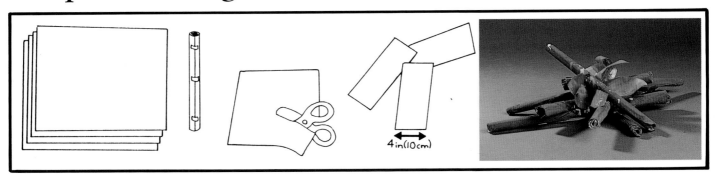

To make the logs, place 4 single sheets of newspaper one on top of the other and roll loosely from the short end. Secure with tape. Make 6 more rolls. Paint the rolls to resemble logs.

To make the fire, paint 5 single sheets of newspaper, one each of red, orange, yellow, green, and blue. Paint one side first. Dry. Turn over and paint the other side. Dry. Cut into strips 4 in (10 cm) wide.

Crumple the strips to represent flames. Pile the logs on top of each other like a campfire, and glue. Place the paper flames between the logs and glue in place as shown.

The planets

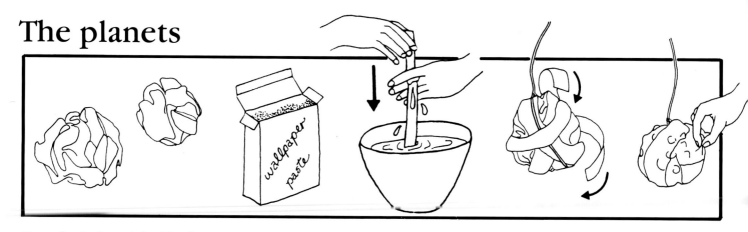

Crumple single and double sheets of newspaper into 10 balls. See different sizes as shown. Cover each ball with strips of newspaper dipped in wallpaper paste and wrapped around the balls to make various sizes for the solar system. Tie a string around each ball before applying the last layer of newspaper stripping.

Leave 3 ft (1 m) of string to hang the finished planet. (See diagram. Illustrations are not to scale.)

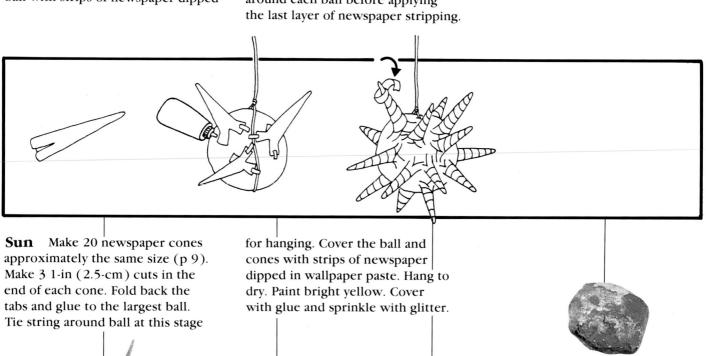

Sun Make 20 newspaper cones approximately the same size (p 9). Make 3 1-in (2.5-cm) cuts in the end of each cone. Fold back the tabs and glue to the largest ball. Tie string around ball at this stage for hanging. Cover the ball and cones with strips of newspaper dipped in wallpaper paste. Hang to dry. Paint bright yellow. Cover with glue and sprinkle with glitter.

Earth Choose a ball the same size as Venus. Hang to dry. Paint oceans and continents and polar ice cap.

Venus Choose a slightly larger ball than for Mercury. Hang to dry. Paint blue/green.

Mercury Choose the smallest ball, Hang to dry. Paint medium yellow.

 Sun   Mercury   Venus   Earth   Mars   Jupiter    Saturn   Uranus Neptune Pluto

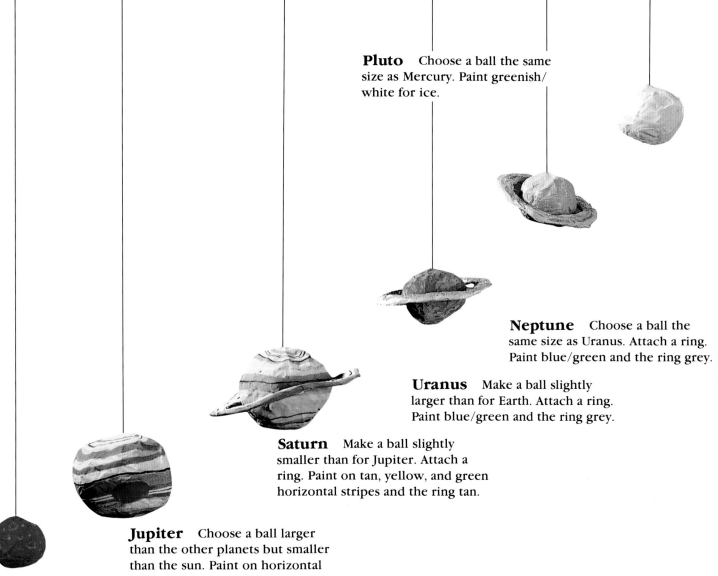

Pluto Choose a ball the same size as Mercury. Paint greenish/white for ice.

Neptune Choose a ball the same size as Uranus. Attach a ring. Paint blue/green and the ring grey.

Uranus Make a ball slightly larger than for Earth. Attach a ring. Paint blue/green and the ring grey.

Saturn Make a ball slightly smaller than for Jupiter. Attach a ring. Paint on tan, yellow, and green horizontal stripes and the ring tan.

Jupiter Choose a ball larger than the other planets but smaller than the sun. Paint on horizontal stripes with one red spot.

Mars Choose a ball smaller than for Earth. Paint red with craters.

Rings for 3 planets

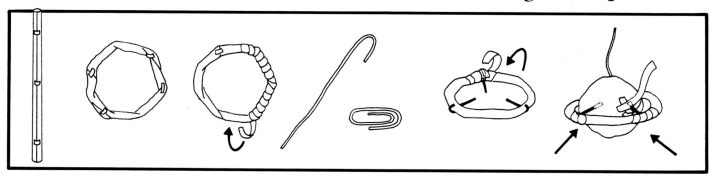

Roll a single sheet of newspaper from the long side. Tape closed. Bend the tube into a circle to fit around the planet, leaving a space between the ring and the planet. Secure ends of the ring. Make 3 of these: one each for Saturn, Neptune, and Uranus. Wrap the ring with newspaper strips dipped in wallpaper paste. Unfold 3 paper clips for each of the planets, leaving one hook in each paper clip as shown. Hook the paper clips around the ring and push the straight ends of the paper clips into the ball planet as shown. Cover the paper clips with newspaper strips dipped in wallpaper paste. Support the rings with crumpled newspaper until they are dry. They are then solid and will hang freely.

Rocket ship and launching area

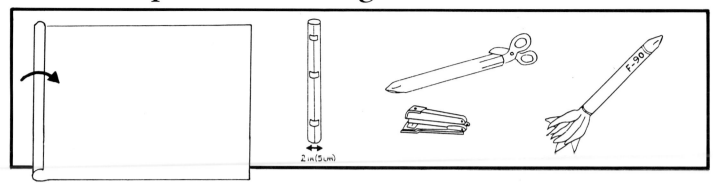

To make the rocket ship, roll loosely a single sheet of newspaper from the short end. Tape along the side. Rolled tube should measure about 2 in (5 cm) in diameter. Fold one end of the tube to a point and staple. This is the nose cone. Make 5 evenly spaced cuts 6 in (15 cm) deep in the other end of the tube. Paint the fringed end of the rocket in reds, yellows, oranges, to resemble booster flames. Paint the remainder of the rocket silver. Cut out numbers and letters from a newspaper for the rocket markings. Glue on.

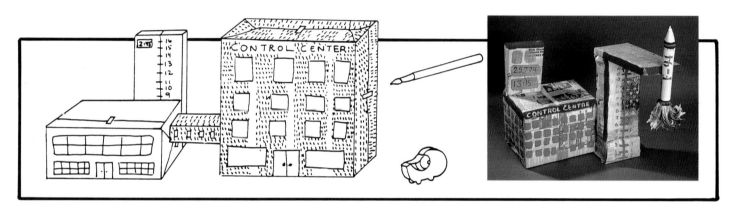

For the *launching area,* wrap large boxes with sheets of newspaper. Paint and decorate with felt markers to resemble buildings.

Mountain scene

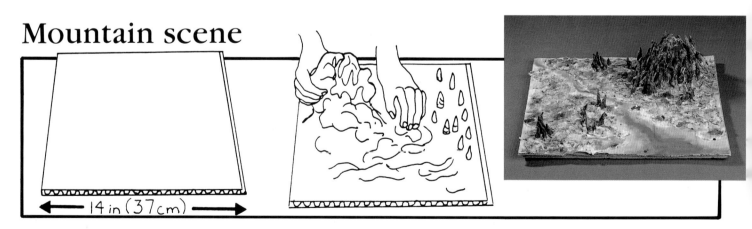

Use a 14 in (37 cm) square of firm cardboard for the base and create a scene from papier-mâché pulp (p 14). Crumple a newspaper for a mountain. Place on the base and cover with papier-mâché pulp. Allow a space for the lake. Attach trees and tiny animals of your choice molded from papier-mâché pulp. Allow to dry.

Paint appropriate colors.

Dandelions, chrysanthemums, carnations

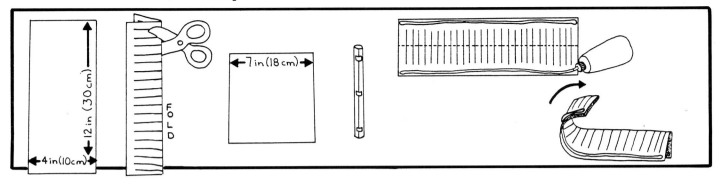

Cut a piece of newspaper 4 in (10 cm) by 12 in (30 cm). Paint one side bright yellow for a dandelion. (Paint other types of flowers pink, purple, red, or pale yellow.) When

dry, fold in half lengthwise, painted side out. Cut in 1.5 in (4 cm) along the folded edge at regular intervals to make a fringe as shown. Set aside. Roll a 7 in (18 cm) square of

newspaper into a tight tube for a stem. Glue edges and tape. Using the fringed strip, unfold the paper and put glue on the long unfringed edges of both sides as shown. Fold closed again. Begin

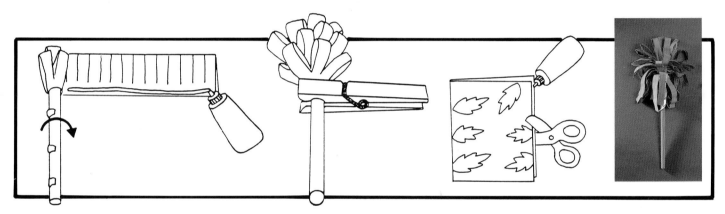

wrapping the fringed strip tightly around one end of the stem as shown. As you wrap, a fat flower begins to take shape. A clothespin will hold it together as it dries.

When dry, fold the fringes down, one by one, for petals.
Fold a single sheet of newspaper in half and glue together. Draw

leaves. Cut out and glue to flower stem. Allow to dry. Paint green.

Tulips, crocuses, sunflowers, daisies

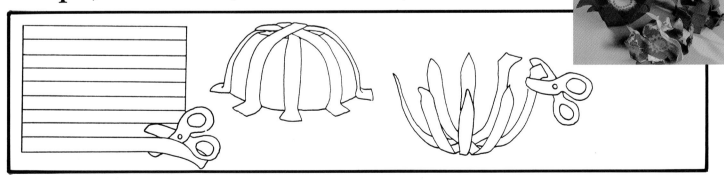

Using a slab of papier-mâché (p 13), cut the wet slab into strips 2 in (5 cm) wide. Lay the wet strips over an inverted bowl or dish mold,

alternating the direction of the strips. When dry, remove "flower" from the bowl, trim the petals to points, and paint.

ANIMAL KINGDOM

Sheep

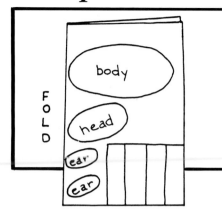  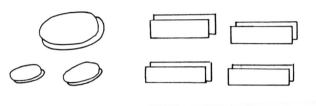

Fold a double sheet of newspaper along the crease. Draw 4 ovals: one for the body 5 in by 8 in (12 cm by 20 cm), one for the head 1.5 in by 3 in (4 cm by 7.5 cm), 2 for the ears 1 in by 2 in (2.5 cm by 5 cm). Cut out. Cut 4 strips of newspaper for the legs 3 in by 0.5 in (7.5 cm by 1 cm). Place the same-sized ovals and strips, one on top of the other, and glue together as shown.

 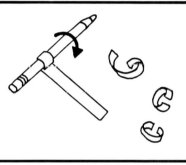

Glue legs to make 2 Xs. Glue Xs to the bottom of the oval body. Glue the head oval to one end of the body. Glue the ears, pointing downward, to the head, one on each side of the head.
Cut many strips of newspaper 0.5 in by 2 in (1 cm by 5 cm). Curl each strip around a pencil. Glue the curled strips all over the sheep's body for wool. Add a small

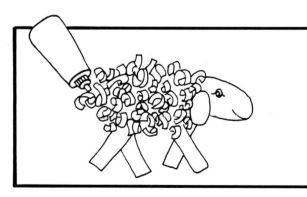 

newspaper curl for the tail. Paint on eyes and a smile.

Dinosaur

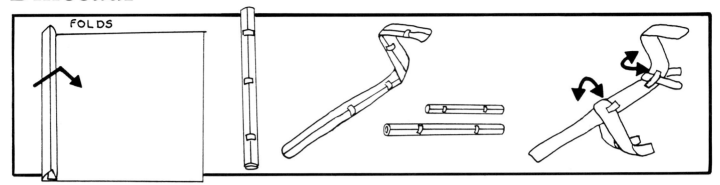

Fold a single sheet of newspaper from long edge in 1 in (2.5 cm) folds, over and over. Tape.

Bend one-third of the roll upwards for the neck. Bend a head down from the end of the neck as shown. The remainder will be the body and tail.

Fold another single sheet of newspaper in the same way for the back legs. Cut a single sheet in half and fold for the front legs. Bend them over the body for the front legs and back legs as shown, and tape in place.

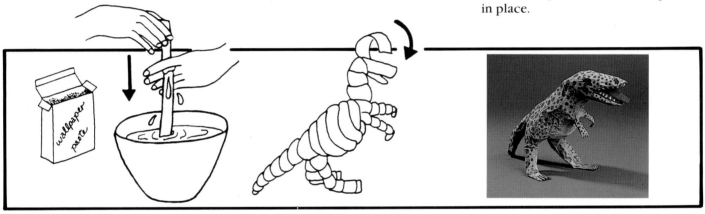

Cover the entire dinosaur figure with strips of newspaper dipped in wallpaper paste, modeling the figure with your hands as you apply the strips to make the desired shape.

Allow several days to dry before painting.
Camels, buffalos, anteaters, giraffes can also be made using this technique. Depending on the

animal you are making, build up bumps and humps with crumpled newspaper fastened on and covered with strips of newspaper dipped in wallpaper paste.

Small people

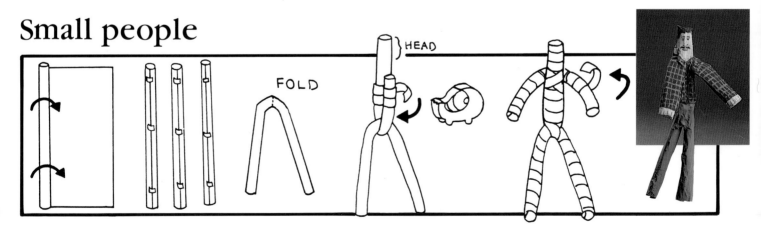

Make 3 tightly rolled newspaper tubes (p 8), each 12 in (30 cm) long. Fold each tube in half as shown. Loop one tube around the other tube like a chain link to make

the torso and legs of a person as shown, leaving about 1 in (2.5 cm) sticking up for the head. Tape torso area securely.

Wrap the third roll around the torso to make the arms. Tape. Cover the entire figure with strips of newspaper dipped in wallpaper paste. Allow to dry. Paint.

Lion head

Fold a double sheet of newspaper along the crease. Fold in half again from the short end. Draw a lion head outline on the top layer. Cut out. You will have 4 shapes.

Glue one shape on top of the other. Paint a friendly or fierce face on the lion.
Cut many strips of newspaper 0.5 in by 2 in (1 cm by 5 cm). Curl

the strips around a pencil. Glue the curls around the lion's face for the mane.

Elephant head

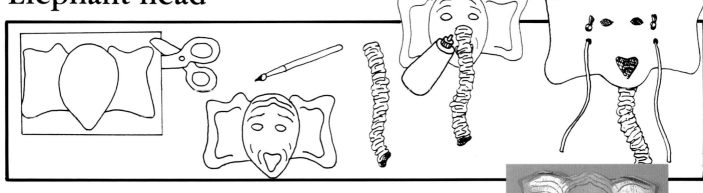

Make a papier-mâché slab (p 13). Draw an elephant head shape on top of the slab. Cut out. Dry. Paint features for an elephant as shown. Make a trunk from a crushed news-

paper tube (p 10). Glue it to the face of the elephant. Paint. If you wish to make a mask, cut out holes for the eyes and mouth. Attach string to sides to hold the mask in place.

Fish

Use a plastic pop bottle for the base. Cover completely with papier-mâché pulp (p 14). When covered, shape the pulp with your fingers

into rough scales all over the body as shown. Add more pulp to shape the tail and fins. Allow to dry. Paint. Add buttons for the eyes.

Spider

From a single sheet of newspaper draw 3 circles 6 in (15 cm) in diameter and many strips 0.5 in by 2 in (1 cm by 5 cm). Cut out. Glue the circles one on top of the other. Curl each strip around a pencil as shown.

Glue one end of each strip to the top of the circle. This makes the spider's furry body.

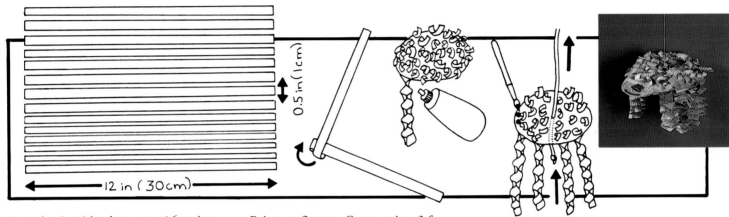

To make 8 spider legs, use 16 strips of newspaper, each 0.5 in by 12 in (1 cm by 30 cm). Make catstairs using 2 strips for each leg (p 11). Glue the legs to the bottom of the spider's body, 4 on each side of the circle.

Paint on 2 eyes. Cut a string 3 ft (1 m) long and thread one end through a darning needle. Poke through the center of the spider's body, take out needle, and knot string. Use free end for hanging.

Caterpillar

Make a crushed newspaper tube (p 10). Paint a face on one end. Paint the rest of the body yellow with black dots.

Fold a double sheet of newspaper in half and glue. Fold in half again. Draw 10 feet on the top sheet as shown. Cut out through both layers.

You should have 10 pairs of feet. Glue the feet to each side of the body. Paint the feet purple.

Frog

To make a large frog, use a medium-sized cardboard box for the body and head, 2 shoebox lids for the feet, and 2 jewelry boxes for eyes. Tape the shoebox lids to the edge of the larger box, one on each side as shown. Tape the jewelry boxes near the front of the large box for eyes as shown. Add a triangular shaped piece of cardboard to the back of the large box for a tail. Poke holes in front of the eyes for nostrils.

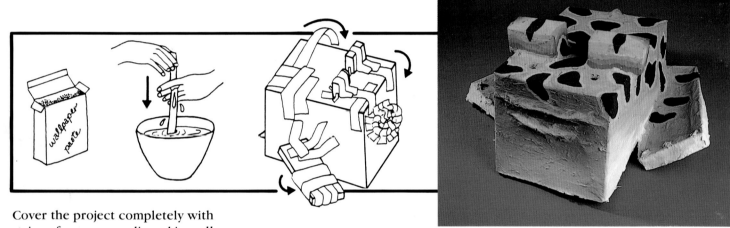

Cover the project completely with strips of newspaper dipped in wallpaper paste. For lips, build up the front area with strips of newspaper dipped in paste. Allow to dry. Paint.

Snake

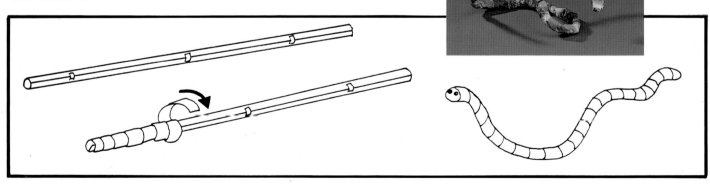

Make a long newspaper tube (p 8). Cover with strips of newspaper dipped in wallpaper paste. While still wet and pliable, bend the covered tube into a snake shape. Allow to dry. Paint.

Turkey

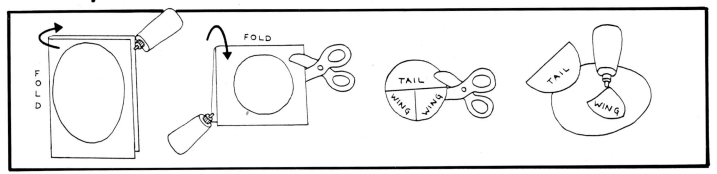

Fold one double sheet of newspaper along the crease and glue together. Fold one single sheet of newspaper in half short end to short end and glue together. When dry, cut out a

large oval 23 in by 13 in (58 cm by 33 cm) from the larger sheet and a circle 10 in (25 cm) in diameter from the smaller sheet.
Cut the circle in half. Glue one

half to the turkey body for the tail as shown. Cut the remaining half in half again. Glue to the body for wings, curved side downward as shown.

Draw a turkey head and 2 feet on a single sheet of newspaper. Make head and feet an appropriate size to suit the body. Cut out. Glue to the turkey. Paint.

Cut many small strips of newspaper 0.5 in by 2 in (1 cm by 5 cm) and curl around a pencil (p 10). Glue to the turkey body for feathers.

Paint a small piece of newspaper red. When dry, crumple for a wattle. Glue under turkey head.

Rabbit

Using about one cup of papier-mâché pulp (p 14), mold pulp into a rabbit shape with your hands.

Mold points for ears, a lump for the tail, and lumps for arms and feet. Allow to dry. Paint.

Parrot in a cage

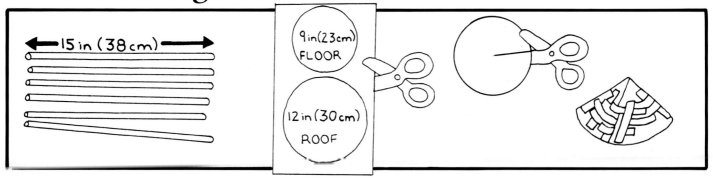

Make 6 tightly rolled slim news-paper tubes (p 8), each 15 in (38 cm) long.
Make a papier-mâché slab from 6 single sheets of newspaper (p 13) dipped in wallpaper paste. While

still wet, cut out 2 circles from this slab, one 9 in (23 cm) in dia-meter and one 12 in (30 cm) in diameter. For the cage roof, make a cone using the larger circle (p 9). Cut in from the edge of the circle

to the center and overlap the ends as shown. Cover with strips of newspaper dipped in wallpaper paste. The smaller circle is the cage floor. Allow to dry.

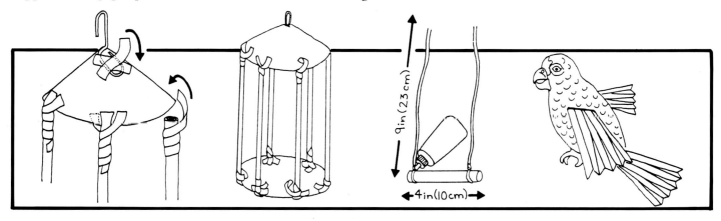

Attach the tubes to the roof and floor of the cage and secure a paper clip to the center of the roof for a hanging hook, using news-paper strips dipped in wallpaper

paste as shown. Allow to dry. Paint. For a cage swing, make a tightly rolled tube from a piece of newspaper 4 in (10 cm) wide and the length of a single sheet of news-

paper. Tie strings 9 in (23 cm) long around each end of the tube. Make a parrot to fit into the cage. Use the hummingbird technique (p 69).

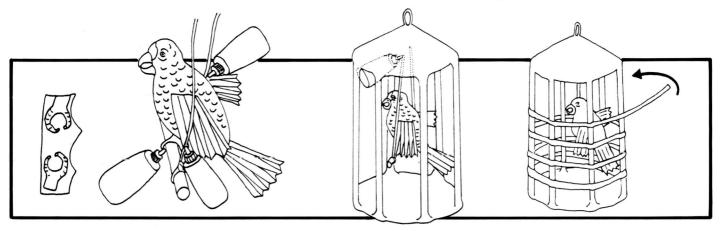

Cut out feet from papier-mâché slab scraps and glue to the bottom of the bird. Paint to look like a parrot. Place the parrot on

the perch swing. Glue the feet to the swing bar and the wings to the swing strings. Carefully secure the swing to the roof of the cage with glue and tape.

Cut 5 strips of newspaper 0.5 in (1 cm) wide and long enough to wrap around the outside of the bars as shown. Glue in place. Paint.

Hummingbird

Draw a bird shape on top of 4 single sheets of newspaper that have been glued together. Cut out.

When dry, cut a slit in the body of the bird where the wings will go.

To make wings, accordion pleat (p 9) an 8 in (20 cm) square piece of newspaper.

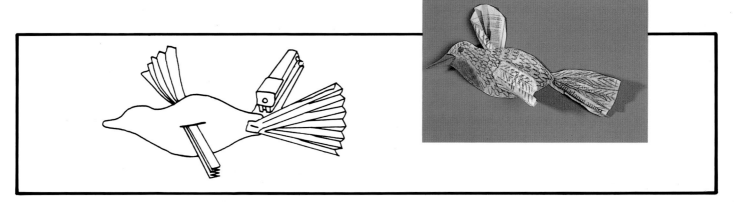

Slip the pleated newspaper wings through the slot in the body, allowing the wings to stick out evenly on both sides. Bend each side of the wings upwards on both sides

of the body and spread out as a fan. Accordion pleat a 6 in (5 cm) square of newspaper for the tail. Staple one end of the folded fan to the end of body. Spread out the unstapled end. Paint.

69

DRESS UP

Pleated tartan

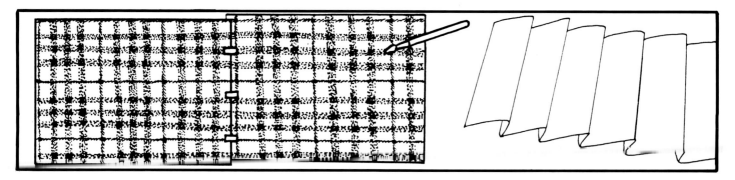

Use 2 double sheets of newspaper, tape or glue short ends together as shown. Paint a tartan pattern of your choice on the newspaper sheets.

You may want to vary the number of sheets for the size of skirt needed. Allow to dry.

Accordion pleat (p 9) with 2 in (5 cm) folds, starting at the short end.

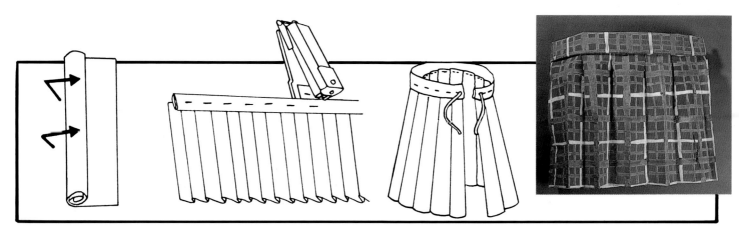

For the waistband, fold a single sheet of newspaper, lengthwise, over and over, 6 times. Staple the waistband onto the pleated sheet along the long edge as shown.

Punch a hole in each end of the waistband. Thread a string through each hole and knot at the inside, leaving a length on the right side of the skirt band to tie. Pin the skirt

part way down with a large safety pin for a kilt.

Belts

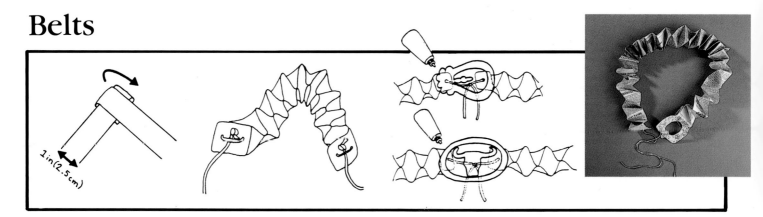

Make a catstair (p 11) 1 in (2.5 cm) wide and the length of the size of the belt required. Knot a string at one end and staple to each end of catstair, leaving enough string on

each side to tie the belt. Fold up catstair and paint the edges if you wish. Make a belt buckle from a piece of papier-mâché slab (p 13). Cut out the desired buckle shape. Paint. Allow

to dry. Decorate with glue sprinkled with glitter. When dry, glue the belt buckle to one end of the catstair belt. Tie the belt strings next to the body behind the belt buckle.

Grass skirt

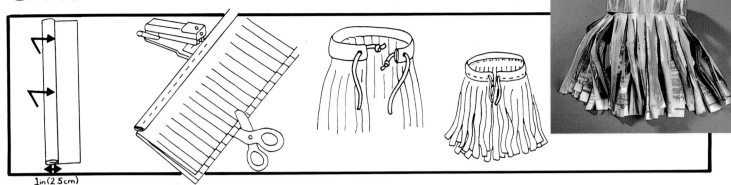

For the waistband, fold a double sheet of newspaper lengthwise 6 times. For the skirt, fold another double sheet along the crease (or 2 double sheets taped at the short end if a larger skirt is required). Glue and

staple the waistband over the sheet at the fold as shown. Paint the outside sheet a grass color.
When dry, make 1-in (2.5-cm)-wide cuts from the bottom edge of the skirt to within 1 in (2.5 cm) of the

waistband as shown. Punch a hole in each end of the waistband. Thread a string through each hole and knot the string on the inside, leaving a length on the outside to tie. Wrap the skirt around the waist. Tie the waistband.

Hawaiian leis   Method 1

Cut several newspapers into 12 in (30 cm) squares. Crumple each square into a ball.

Using a darning needle threaded with strong string, poke through each crumpled ball and thread onto the string to form a long

necklace. When the desired length is reached, remove the needle and tie the ends of the string together. Paint to resemble flowers.

Method 2

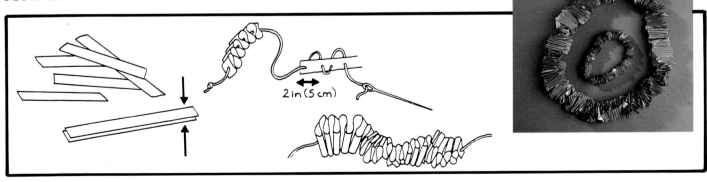

Cut long strips of newspaper 2 in (5 cm) wide. Place one strip on top of the other for fullness. *Do not glue together.*

Thread a darning needle with strong string and tie a large knot at one end. Sew in and out through the newspaper strips as shown, taking 2 in (5 cm) stitches each time.

Continue to thread until the lei is the desired length. Remove needle, tie ends of string together. Paint to resemble flowers.

Angel wings

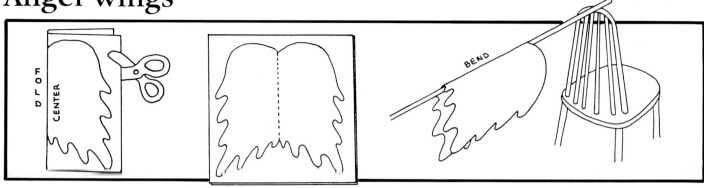

Fold a single sheet of newspaper in half. Draw a pattern for the wings using the folded edge as the center as shown. Cut out and unfold. The size of the wings is determined by the size of the child who will wear them.

Place this wing pattern on a wet slab of papier-mâché (p 13). The pattern will stick to the slab. Cut out. Peel off pattern and discard.

While wet, bend wings upwards and position as desired. Hang the wings over a chair back or rod until dry. Paint and decorate with glue sprinkled with glitter. Poke 2 holes

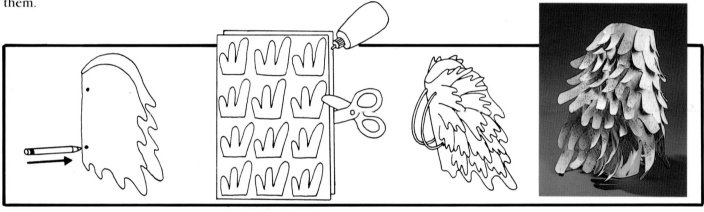

on either side of the center of the wings as shown. Pull 2 strings through the holes and knot the strings on the inside of the wings. The child can put his or her arms

through the strings and wear the wings on the back (see diagram). For feathers, glue together 2 single sheets of newspaper. Allow to dry.

Draw 12 feather shapes on the top layer as shown. Cut out. This makes enough feathers for one wing. Repeat for the other wing. Paint. Glue to wings.

To make a halo

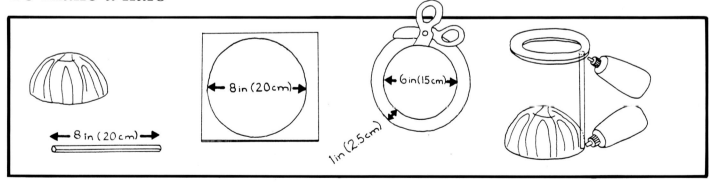

Select a kitchen bowl the approximate size of the child's head and make a newspaper bowl (p 20). For the halo ring, make a papier-mâché slab (p 13), draw a circle 8 in (20 cm) in diameter and cut

out. Draw a circle 6 in (15 cm) in diameter inside the first circle and cut out, leaving a 1 in (2.5 cm) ring. Make a tightly rolled tube 8 in (20 cm) long. Glue edges. Glue the top end of tube to the flat of

the ring as shown. Glue the other end of the tube to the newspaper bowl as shown. Cover with newspaper strips dipped in wallpaper paste. When dry, paint. Cover with glue and sprinkle with glitter.

Masks   Basic shape

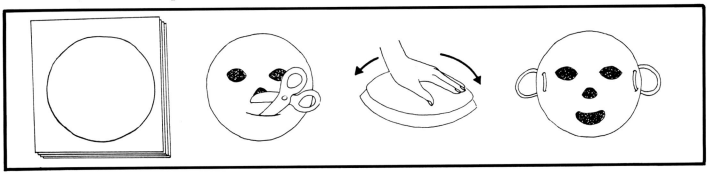

Make a 4-sheet papier-mâché slab (p 13). While wet, cut an oval or circle or square or rectangle, whichever best suits the kind of mask you wish to make, large enough

to cover the child's face. While the slab is wet, also cut out holes for eyes, nose, and mouth. Then press and shape the mask on an inverted plate. Allow to dry.

Poke 2 holes on each side of the mask. Loop a piece of string at each side through the 2 holes and knot on the inside of the mask, leaving enough string to fit over the wearer's ears.

Face masks

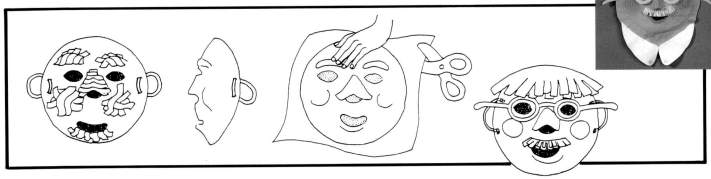

Add crumpled balls of newspaper to the front of the mask to give contours to the face. Hold in place with strips of newspaper dipped in wallpaper paste.
Press strips gently around bumps

and humps. Coat the mask with paste. Lay a piece of tissue paper over the mask and smooth gently all over and through the holes as shown. This will give a finished texture.

When dry, trim off the excess tissue paper. Paint, shellac, and decorate. For an old man mask, cut out fringed sheets of newspaper (p 10) for hair and mustache. Glue to mask. Cut out a pair of glasses and glue to mask as shown. Paint if desired.

Body masks

Make a 6-sheet papier-mâché slab (p 13). Draw the desired pattern on the slab such as the wallpaper and portrait shown here. Cut out.

Cut out a hole for the child's face to show through. Allow to dry. Paint. See tiger body mask on p 71.

Hats   Basic shape

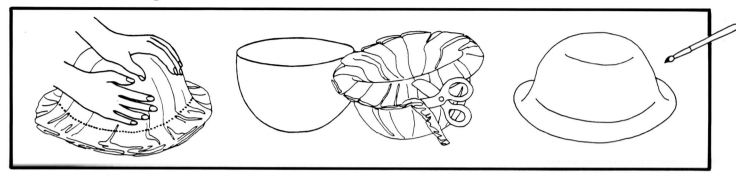

Make a 6-sheet papier-mâché slab (p 13). Place the wet slab over a deep, head-sized bowl, which has been inverted on a flat surface.

Press the slab firmly over the bowl. Allow to dry.

When dry, remove the bowl and trim the edges. Paint and shellac. The basic hat shape is now ready for decoration.

Dinosaur hat

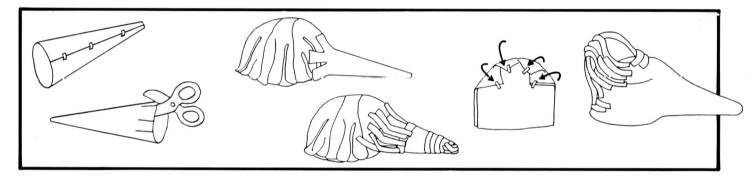

For the snout, fold a single sheet of newspaper in half, roll into a cone (p 9), tape. Make 3 cuts in the base and attach it to one side of a basic hat shape as shown, using newspaper strips dipped in

wallpaper paste. Fold over the ends of the snout and flatten the underside of the cone. Wrap with strips dipped in paste.
Fold a double sheet of newspaper into a ridge shape any size you

desire for the back of the hat. Tape to secure the folds. Attach the ridge to the basic hat shape with strips dipped in paste. Continue to cover entire ridge with these strips.

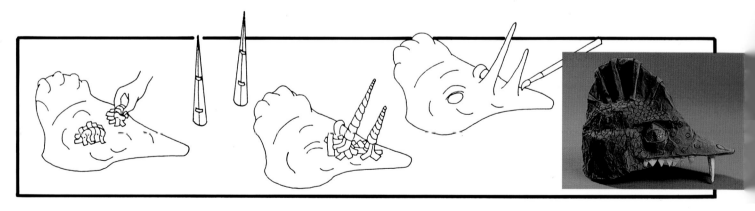

Mold bumps for the lids of bulging eyes from crumpled newspaper. Apply while head shape is still wet with more strips dipped in paste.

Make 2 cones (p 9) for the horns. Make 3 cuts in each base. Attach these with strips dipped in paste. Cover cones as shown.

Dry hat over inverted bowl. Use button technique for eyes (p 11). Glue. Dry. Paint in pupils and decorate.

Crown

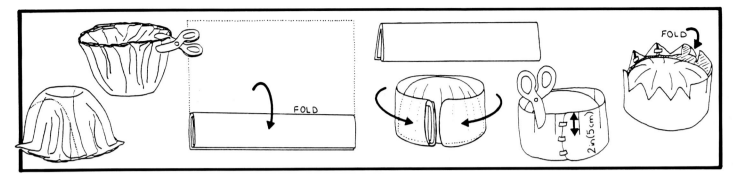

Make a basic hat shape to fit the child's head. Dry. Cut off brim. Paint purple. Set aside. Fold double sheet of newspaper over and over from the long side, using 6 in (15 cm) folds. Tape. Fit around basic hat shape as shown. Tape. Make 2 in (5 cm) cuts around the top, 2 in (5 cm) apart. Fold the sides into the center to make points as shown. Tape. Paint and decorate. See photograph p 78.

Cowboy hat

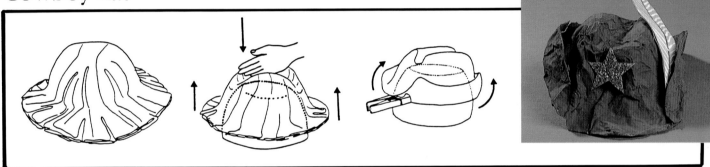

Following the basic hat shape directions (p 76), leave a large brim around the shape on all sides. While wet, lift the hat slightly off the bowl and press in a crease along the top from front to back as shown. Also shape the brim while wet by bending up the sides of the news- paper slab brim as shown. Use clothespins, front and back, to hold the brim in place until dry. When dry, paint and decorate.

Nurse's hat

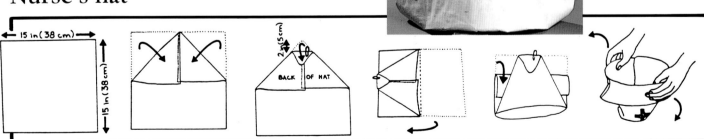

This hat can be made from either a wet papier-mâché slab (p 13) 15 in (38 cm) square or several layers of newspaper (not glued together), also 15 in (38 cm) square. The instructions apply for both versions. Place the square on a flat surface. Fold the top corners towards the center of the square as shown. This is the back of the hat. Tape if using dry newspaper. Fold down top point 2 in (5 cm). Hold closed with a paper clip if using a papier-mâché slab. Tape if using dry newspaper. For the brim, fold the bottom of the square once, toward the front of the hat. Fold over again. Open the hat and place over an inverted bowl to dry if using papier-mâché. Paint.

Shoes

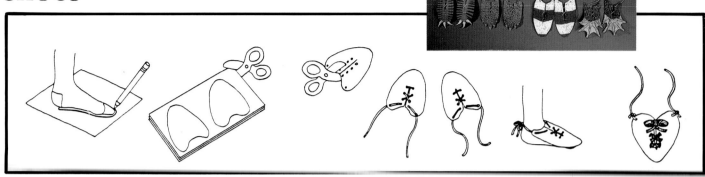

Have the child stand on a piece of newspaper and trace the shape of the front of the foot as shown. Cut out and use for the pattern. Make a 6-sheet papier-mâché slab (p 13). While wet, place the pattern on the slab and cut out. Cut a slit down the center of each cut shape, from the ankle to the toe section, but *do not cut* all the way to the end of the shoe. Punch shoelace holes, 4 down each side of the slit, and one hole at each top corner as shown.

Allow to dry. Paint and decorate. Lace shoes with brightly colored laces, leaving enough lace to tie around the ankle.

Battleshield and spear

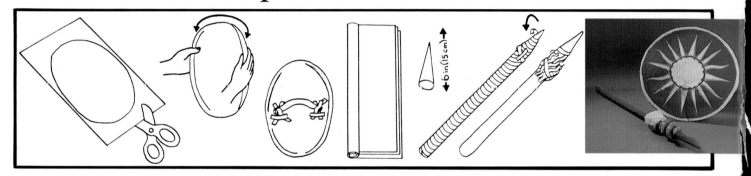

Draw pattern of a shield on a sheet of newspaper. Cut out. Make a 6-sheet papier-mâché slab (p 13). Lay pattern on wet slab. Cut out. Remove pattern. While wet, shape shield. Make a newspaper tube (p 8). Tape to back of shield. Cover with strips of newspaper dipped in wallpaper paste. Dry. Paint. Spear. Place 3 sheets of newspaper, one on top of the other, and make a tight roll. Tape. Cover with strips dipped in paste. Make a cone (p 9) from 6 in (15 cm) square of newspaper. Fit on end of spear. Tape. Cover spear with strips dipped in paste. Add crumpled newspaper for decoration and cover with more strips. Dry. Paint.

Sword and crown

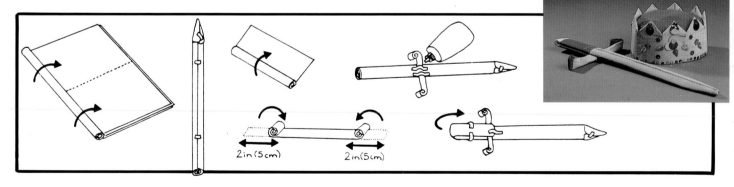

Place 3 double sheets of newspaper one on top of the other. Roll from the long side as shown. Glue loose edges and tape. Flatten the roll. Fold the corners of one end to make a point. Glue and tape. Roll up a single sheet of newspaper from the short end. Glue the loose edge. Flatten the ends and roll each up 2 in (5 cm) as shown. Tape. Turn on its side and flatten the middle of this roll. This is the handle guard. Place the handle guard 12 in (30 cm) from the end of the larger tube and tape in place. Fold up the end of the larger tube so that it lies over the guard as shown. Glue and tape. This forms the handle. When the glue is dry, remove the tape and paint.

Turtle shell costume

Cut out 3 large oval shapes 6 in (15 cm) long from stiff cardboard for the center of the upper turtle shell. Lay them side by side and tape together as shown. Cut out 4 ovals

5 in (12 cm) long from stiff cardboard, and tape around first 3 circles, overlapping the edges as shown.

Cut out 15 ovals 3 in (8 cm) long from cardboard and place around the other circles. Tape, overlapping edges slightly as shown.

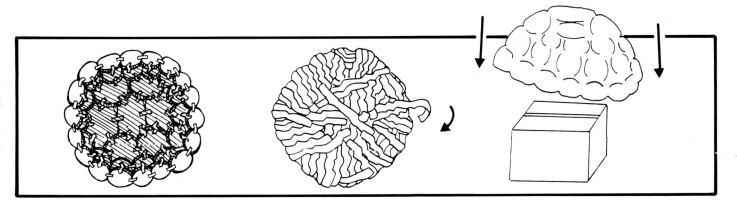

Cut additional ovals 3 in (8 cm) long and place them around the circle, overlapping the edges slightly. Tape, turn over. Cover this underside with sheets and strips of

newspaper dipped in wallpaper paste. Place the center circles over a cardboard box with the covered side down and let the rest of the cardboard circle drape over the

sides to form a dome. Cover the top with sheets of newspaper dipped in wallpaper paste. Allow to dry. Remove from box.
For the turtle tummy cut a turtle

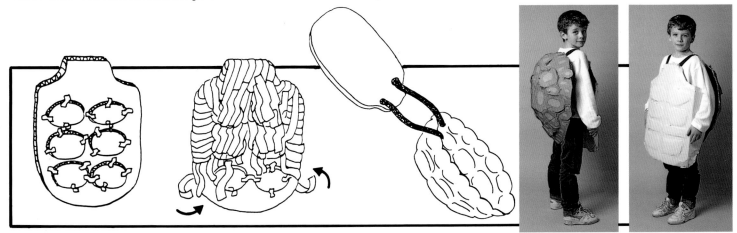

shape from a sheet of stiff cardboard to match the size of the upper shell. From another sheet of cardboard cut out 6 ovals, 6 in (15 cm) long and tape to the top of the cardboard shape as shown.

Cover this side with more newspaper sheets and strips dipped in wallpaper paste. Shape the bottom shell while wet by bending the outer edges in slightly. Allow to dry.

Poke holes in the upper and lower shells to attach ropes or straps as shown. The straps will rest on the child's shoulders.
Paint.

Index